Secret
MEN'S
BBQ
BUSINESS

Secret

MEN'S
BBQ
BUSINESS

The Complete Guide to Barbecuing

ALLAN CAMPION

Hardie Grant Books

First published in 2002
by Hardie Grant Books
12 Claremont Street
South Yarra,Victoria 3141, Australia
www.hardiegrant.com.au

National Library of Australia Cataloguing-in-Publication Data:

Campion, Allan.
Secret men's BBQ business.
Includes index.
ISBN 1 74064 105 1.
1. Barbecue cookery – Australia. 2. Barbecues (Fireplaces).
I. Title.
641.76

Edited by Dale Campisi
Cover and text design by Phil Campbell
Typeset by J & M Typesetting
Printed and bound in Australia by Griffin Press

*To Michele, who occasionally prises the tongs
from my hands (and does a mighty fine job
of barbecuing when she does).*

CONTENTS

My backyard barbie   viii

PART 1 – THE DRILL

From caveman to snag   2

Barbecues historically, in Australia and
around the world

Size does matter   12

Choosing a barbecue for your backyard

Hammer and tongs   20

Building your own barbecue

The power of the tongs and   28
other sacred objects

Barbecue tools and utensils

The secret's in the sizzle   33

Firing up and cleaning up

The barbecue cook's pantry   39

Ingredients for flavour and success

Working up a thirst   48

Barbecues, beer and wine

PART 2 – THE GRILL

Barbecue golden rules   58

The skill of the grill   61

Setting up, choosing your prey,
the big lesson and serving up

Spice mixes, marinades   65
and bastes

Cooking sausages and burgers   73

Cooking on the bone   84

Cooking kebabs   97

Cooking the perfect steak   111

Cooking whole things   128

The spit roast   147

Vegetarian food   154

Salads   163

Salsas, chutneys, sauces and mustard   172

Desserts   180

List of recipes by sections   189

MY BACKYARD BARBIE

The barbecue in my backyard is neither new nor packed with the latest accessories. It doesn't have a wok burner, built-in rotisserie or even a roasting dish. The automatic ignition stopped working ages ago and a few of the gas jets are a bit dodgy, to say the least. It may look a bit shabby and worn out after four years in the great outdoors but it's mine, all mine – and I love it.

Despite my barbecue's aesthetic and technological shortcomings, I love it because we share an understanding. I know its hot and cold spots; I know the noises it makes when it hits just the right temperature for cooking. In return, I clean it well after use, keep it filled with gas and give it a proper service before retiring it to the garage for winter.

It's at the barbecue that I feel most comfortable and completely in control. It's my undisputed 'spot' in the backyard where, with tongs in hand, I cook and provide for family and friends. It's where I chat with my mates, sometimes about food but generally about life.

I have been fascinated with barbecuing (and indeed, with the psychology of barbecuing) for some time now – about how it fits into Australian social and culinary culture; and why men have taken up the tongs when traditionally women have done most household cooking.

My first exploration of these ideas was published in *Sizzle! Modern Barbecue Food* a few years ago, which I co-wrote with my partner Michele Curtis. While working on this book, we also developed the idea, along with Ian Scott, that Australia should have a national day to celebrate barbecuing. This idea evolved into National BBQ Day, which is held on the last Sunday of November every year.

I hope you enjoy this latest addition to the modern man's culture that is the Australian barbecue. May it give you much food for thought.

ALLAN CAMPION

THE AUSTRALIAN BARBECUE OATH

I do solemnly swear that from this day
forward I will uphold the natural right
of all men to cook at the barbecue.
I promise to keep control of the tongs
at all times and I will gladly pass on all
the secrets I know about the skill of the
grill to younger blokes.

Part 1

THE DRILL

FROM CAVEMAN TO SNAG

Throughout history man has been the hunter, bread-winner and provider for his family. He's been master of his domain – the undisputed head of the family unit and creator of offspring. Well, bugger me if things haven't turned pear-shaped in the past couple of decades.

Recent times have seen incredible changes to man's role in society. Nowadays, both men and women go out to work; do the cooking and cleaning; take the littlies to kinder gym; change nappies; wash the dishes; do the school drop-offs; spend quality time with the kiddies and even do the shopping. And as if that's not enough, the wonders of modern medical research have virtually rendered men redundant to human reproduction.

Much of this change can be attributed to the arrival of the Sensitive New Age Guy and the advent of Political Correctness – trends that make mere males tremble with fear. How the hell does this relate to barbecuing? We'll get to that bit in a minute.

Just as there are trends where blokes are expected to turn into PC SNAGs, it's also inevitable that there'll be a male-driven backlash against these developments. This is not to say that men want to turn back the clock totally (well some do). It's more about finding a balance and allowing the real man inside to emerge. This manifests itself in various ways – including the advent of wild man weekends, where busloads of

The barbecue is just the thing modern man needs to keep his manhood on track.

blokes head into the bush to hug trees and perform ancient manly rituals while dancing around log fires and howling like dingoes into the night sky.

I'm here to tell you that the path to releasing the real man inside you is a lot closer than a $250, three-day bush safari. In fact, it's right under your nose in your own backyard. Yep, the barbecue is just the thing modern man needs to keep his manhood on track. The reasoning behind this theory is simple. All we need is a brief history lesson on the evolution of the barbecue – from char-grilled mastodon to soy and ginger salmon kebabs.

Imagine the scene if you will: hundreds of thousands of years ago – give or take a millennium or two – a group of Neanderthal men come home from a day's hunting. The clan gathers around to inspect the kill, skin the animals and dish out the evening meal. When everyone has had their fill of raw meat, the leftovers are stored high in a tree to ensure sabre-toothed tigers or other wild animals don't make off with the booty. Finally, the tribe can settle down for some evening respite in their deluxe cave-conversion.

But then: disaster. A powerful storm breaks with a violent crash of lightning, striking the meat-laden tree and setting it aflame. By the next morning, the tree is reduced to a mass of glowing coals and the meat was almost charred beyond recognition.

I'm not sure who was first to try it – probably the oldest, most expendable member of the clan – but the change in flavour and texture was easily noticed, even preferred by some members of the clan. This was Earths' first ever barbecue.

We prehistoric barbecue researchers believe this day to have occurred on the last Sunday of the Neanderthal equivalent of our November – which is why we commemorate National BBQ Day at this time.

Whether or not my Palaeolithic research is based in fact is not the issue, which basically means I can't be proven wrong (a boon, I know)! What we do know is that prehistoric man discovered that he could transform raw meat into something much more palatable by cooking it over a fire. With a little trial and error, our ancestors soon realised that cooked meat kept much longer than raw meat, especially if it was done over a smoky fire. Thereafter, it didn't take too long for barbecuing to become central to the culinary life of man as he set out to explore and conquer lands far from his prehistoric origins.

Today the barbecue has become the rallying point of a new trend – one where men are trying to find a balance between helping around the house and allowing their inner man to emerge. I've characterised this trend as the 21st century SNAG – a Sizzling New Age Guy.

Forget wild man weekends in the bush. Instead, get sizzling at the barbecue. Bugger hugging an old eucalypt, hug your barbie. Don't wear native clothing, don your favourite novelty barbeque apron. Don't dance around a campfire thrusting spears in the air, instead pace around the barbie with your trusty barbecue tongs and a tinnie in hand.

Sure, most of us do our 'hunting' at the local butcher's shop and the 'fire' is more likely to be glowing coals or a gas jet burner, but the essence is still the same. There's the unmistakable, smoky aroma wafting over the neighbour's fence and a selection of glistening, bloodied animal parts just waiting to be transformed into dinner table delectables.

In order to make the barbie a success you'll need to tame the coals and be a whiz with the tongs – you could even try beating your chest with your fists if this helps you get in the mood. You'll soon have the family lined up, plate in hand, to receive barbeque haute cuisine. Once again you're king of your domain, provider for your family. And boy, doesn't it feel good?

THE BARBECUE IN AUSTRALIA

Now we come to barbecuing in Australia – famous across the world as the home of the modern barbecue.

The barbecue has come to dominate social interaction and eating habits of Australians like never before. Barbecues abound in virtually every backyard, apartment balcony, suburban park and beachside reserve these days. A barbecue can be a quick meal on a busy weeknight or a huge gathering of family and friends on a Sunday afternoon.

Barbecuing for the Australian man is a delicate mix of masculinity and modernity, with a decent amount of good old-fashioned bravado thrown in. It's also one of the easiest methods of cooking ever invented – there's nothing more than a hot grill and a pair of tongs to think about. Once the barbecue is lit, all the cook has to do is flip a few sausages and lamb chops from time to time.

Compare this to cooking a meal in an indoor kitchen where you have to contend with an array of pots, pans, bowls, knives and wooden spoons, as well as ovens to light, woks to operate and fridges to regulate. It's a hands-down win for the barbecue every time in most bloke's minds because you get maximum flavour from minimum effort, and time to chat with your mates over a cooling ale or two.

To most outsiders, the gathering of men around a barbecue looks completely innocent – but all is not as it seems. There's a whole lot more going on around the hot grill than just sizzling meat. It's at these male-only affairs where the cooking secrets of the barbecue are quietly discussed, where information and advice is passed from man to man and handed down from generation to generation. It's where the Secret Men's Barbecue Business is convened.

To most outsiders, the gathering of men around a barbecue looks completely innocent – but all is not as it seems ... it's where the Secret Men's Barbecue Business is convened.

The barbecue has also become a rite of passage for young Australian men. We're all aware that an eighteen-year-old will need certain things to become a real man: he'll get his licence, his first car, have his first legal beer and surrender his twelfth to a porcelain bus. He'll engage in age-old mating rituals before embarking on the real fun – buying the biggest, meanest barbecue he can afford and wheel it straight into the backyard. Only then is he on the path to becoming a real man.

Then, and only then, can he invite other male members of the tribe to his backyard where they'll gather around the barbecue and pass on all they know about barbecuing. This is what I call the 'skill of the grill' and it's the final rite of passage in the journey from boyhood to manhood for Australian males.

A young barbecue cook's training will see him go through many different phases of enlightenment. He usually begins by learning a few simple marinades and spice mixes before attempting the techniques required to cook small items such as sausages and burgers. Then he'll move onto chops and kebabs, followed by learning how to cook the perfect steak. Then it's onwards and upwards to legs of lamb, whole chickens and fish, and finally onto the Holy Grail of all barbecue cooks – the spit roast.

A young barbecue cook's training will see him go through many different phases of enlightenment before moving onwards and upwards to the Holy Grail of all barbecue cooks – the spit roast.

Now you know the truth about why Australian blokes love barbecuing. It's about rites of passage and asserting manhood in times when the idea of what it is to be a man is difficult to quantify. Men have got their hands firmly on the barbecue tongs and they're not about to hand them over to anyone.

THE BARBECUE AROUND THE WORLD

Many countries around the world have evolved their own distinctive way of barbecuing. Most consider their way of barbecuing to be the one and only way, and that all others are inferior and unauthentic.

Barbecuing has always been most popular in warmer climates: places such as Australia, Africa, North and South America, Asia, the Middle East and Southern Europe. In recent years, however, barbecuing has become increasingly popular in the UK and other parts of central Europe, which begs the question: is there no stopping this phenomenon?

Men have got their hands firmly on the barbecue tongs and they're not about to hand them over to anyone.

The word barbecue originates from the indigenous people of the Caribbean. They preserved meat by drying it in the sun, and in order to keep insects away they lit small fires around the drying meat. The preserved meat – dried and smoky – was referred to as barbacoa, which eventually became barbecue.

Early American settlers developed the preserving technique into smoking pits and smokehouses. People from the southern states of Texas and Carolina, for instance, like nothing more than preparing a huge piece of pork (sometimes beef) by smearing it with a tangy barbecue sauce or rubbing it with a dry spice mixture. The meat is then slow-cooked in a pit until meltingly tender and smoky.

Barbecuing is also incredibly widespread in Spain, Portugal and Greece where fish, cooked over glowing coals, is a popular repast. The Turkish and Lebanese are also barbecuing aficionados. Commonplace dishes include shish kebabs, breads and eggplants cooked over smoky coals until soft, then transformed into the famous baba ghanoush dip.

Genghis Khan, is reputed to have loved nothing more than barbecuing and spit-roasting huge chunks of meat. Maybe we should nominate him as the patron saint of the barbecue.

Across Africa, cooking food over coals is often the only method available. In Morocco, slender meat kebabs spiced with ground cinnamon, paprika, ginger, pepper and saffron are cooked on street-side barbecues and sold as food-on-the-go. In South Africa, the Boer explorers developed a love of cooking meat over open fires and, as a result, the barbecue is still a popular backyard tradition there.

Asian countries have also got their own fair share of barbecuing traditions as well. Thailand, Vietnam and Indonesia have a huge array of meats skewered onto bamboo sticks that are cooked over coals. The satay, made with its distinctive sauce, spices and peanuts is probably the most popular of all. The Sichuan region of China frequently uses smoking and barbecuing as methods of cooking, while the thirteenth century general, Genghis Khan, is reputed to have loved nothing more than barbecuing and spit-roasting huge chunks of meat. Maybe we should nominate him as the patron saint of the barbecue.

While the equipment and flavours of barbecuing have evolved separately (and quite distinctly) around the world, the process of barbecuing meat is still one of the world's most popular ways of cooking.

Barbecuing in Australia today is an amazing multicultural affair. Barbecue cooks are open to try just about any flavours from just about any country around the world. You're as likely to find lamb chops with Thai spices as you are German bratwurst sausages, tandoori chicken and satay beef kebabs on the grill. There's a real openness and interest to new ideas and new foods and it's this, which provides modern Australian barbecue food with an edge over other countries.

SIZE DOES MATTER

CHOOSING A BARBECUE FOR YOUR BACKYARD

Choosing a barbecue is a very important decision. Believe me, size *does* matter. It can be just the thing a bloke needs to lift his moral fibre. It's about showing off your prize possession to a few mates on Saturday arvo when everyone's around to watch the footy. There she sits in all her splendour, sun gleaming off the top, resplendent with tools of the trade, just waiting for the man-of-the-house to come out and to show us what he's really made of.

But the journey from boyhood to manhood is often difficult and full of challenges – such as the blonde chick at the barbecue retailer who just doesn't understand that there's more at stake than just being able to cook a few sausages. For some blokes, the mere thought of walking through the aisles of gleaming barbecues and stainless steel outdoor cooking kitchens is enough to inspire absolute fear. Which appliance will it be? The ever-popular wooden trolley barbecue, the lure of the kettle barbecue, or the thrill of the chase with a *real* barbecue, the open fire?

There she sits in all her splendour, sun gleaming off the top, resplendent with tools of the trade, just waiting for the man-of-the-house to come out and to show us what he's really made of.

━━ ━━ ━━ ━━ ━━ ━━ ━━ ━━ ━━ ━━ ━━ ━━ ━━ ━━

It's a tough choice, no doubt about it. Some men choose to play it safe and allow their other half to have some part in this decision (just to keep the peace you know). Other men will just head straight out and buy the biggest, flashiest and most expensive model they can find and have it all up and running to surprise wifey on her return from the weekend shopping spree. It's hard work to keep the manly pride intact after all.

There comes, of course, the moment of glory when you have to part with some hard-earned cash and buy the beast that will transform you into a man. To help with this important choice, here is my essential guide to the ins and outs of the three main barbecuing methods: the trolley, the kettle and the open-fire barbecue.

TROLLEY BARBECUES

It seems to be every man's dream, the trolley barbecue. Not too much can go wrong: it can be moved with ease from garden to patio at will, or left in pole position, depending on your inclination.

They're convenient and speedy too. Connect the bottle, turn them on and away you go. For the 21st century SNAG, there's also the challenge of erecting the trolley yourself. With some badly translated instructions, an Allen key and around five hours, this new toy can be constructed at home. Alternatively, you may wish to save your self-respect and pay the guy in the shop to do it for you.

The details

- The frame can be either timber or metal. Stainless, solid steel or cast aluminium constructions will last longer in the great outdoors.

- It should have an easily accessible pullout drip tray, strong wheels, and an automatic ignition.

- Ensure your barbecue has both a flat plate and a grill.

- Ensure there are at least two burners under the grill and plate to allow for different cooking temperatures.

- A pull-down lid is excellent if you want to get into barbecuing whole turkeys, pieces of pork or large fish.

- Choose a barbecue that has small benches on each end: these are essential for holding meats, utensils, oil and plates as you cook.

- Choose a barbecue with 3–4 cm walls around the edge to prevent food from rolling off.

- If your trolley barbecue is to be parked in a relatively permanent position, you can get your local gas company to connect a direct gas line to your barbecue. This will avoid the embarrassment of the gas bottle running out.

Optional extras

If money is no object, trolley barbecues can be fitted with rotisseries, woks and roasting dishes. These are excellent for showing off to your mates and would, in barbecuing utopia, be standard issue.

With some badly translated instructions, an Allen key and around five hours, this new toy can be constructed at home. Alternatively, you may wish to save your self-respect and pay the guy in the shop to do it for you.

— — — — — — — — — — — — — —

KETTLE BARBECUES

Kettle barbecues are like brunettes. Maybe not at first glance as attractive as blondes, but with persistence and a little bit of hard work they will turn out to be your faithful cooking assistant.

Kettle barbecues need to be cajoled as they require slavish amounts of time to light the fire and prepare for cooking. This is ideal for the bloke who likes to spend the entire morning preparing the barbecue for lunch. Smelling of smoke and covered in ash, you can legitimately spend the entire morning fiddling with firelighters, matches and flames. Should the wife inquire as to when you're coming in to help with the salads, you can quite honestly say 'when the barbie's lit', and while away another hour or more uninterrupted.

The kettle barbecue is perfect for showing your mother-in-law on Christmas Day what a good husband you are by cooking the turkey to perfection. The Sunday roast will never be the same again either, as potatoes, pumpkin and large joints of meat can

Kettle barbecues are like brunettes. Maybe not at first glance as attractive as blondes, but with persistence and a little bit of hard work they will turn out to be your faithful cooking assistant.

■ ■ ■ ■ ■ ■ ■ ■ ■ ■ ■ ■ ■ ■ ■

come in for this no-holds-barred type of cooking. It's called keeping everyone happy.

While not as big and flashy as some of the trolley barbecues, kettle barbecues are great for the man-about-town, for the city apartment balcony or town-house courtyard. Things are getting easier too as you can now purchase kettle barbecues that can be hooked up to gas bottles. And for the fashion-conscious male, these barbecues come in a wide range of colours, shapes and sizes.

My advice is to do as I do and own both a kettle and a trolley barbecue, space permitting. You can cover all bases and cooking methods then, and have two bar-becues operating at once to really impress your mates.

The details

- Look for a sturdy barbecue. It is not meant to wobble.

- It needs cleaning vents to easily remove ash.

- It also needs a tight-fitting lid.

Optional extras

Endless amounts of accessories such as smoking chips, potato holders, gas fittings and special cooking trays are available.

OPEN-FIRE BARBECUES

It can be as simple as a pile of bricks and a metal rack, or as complicated as a wood-fired oven, but this is it: real barbecuing over a real fire. Wusses and wimps stay well clear – an open-fire barbecue is real men's work.

An open-fire requires dedication, love and lots of time. From lighting the fire and maintaining the heat source, to keeping the little tykes away and sustaining a vigil. This allows a bloke to spend quality time with his barbecue – and his mates. Not only does it improve a male's ego, it does wonders for the food, achieving flavours that trolley and kettle cooks can only ever dream of.

Wusses and wimps stay well clear – an open-fire barbecue is real men's work.

Having a barbecue of this type also means you'll get the chance to drive around your suburb collecting firewood. This is excellent practice for the ultimate barbecue – the spit roast.

Open-fire barbecues also come with the occasional RDO. These are total fire ban days when you'll have to revert to a safer source of heat, such as the gas-powered trolley barbie if you plan on cooking outdoors.

The details

- Use wood or charcoal, or a mixture of both.

- Always allow flames to die down and cook only over the red embers.

- Different types of wood will produce different flavours.

- Never use treated wood, as the fumes can be poisonous.

HAMMER AND TONGS

BUILDING YOUR OWN BARBECUE

I hate to be the bearer of bad news – particularly such a bitter pill – but brothers there are *very* few ways to gain an advantage over other male barbecue fanatics. Short of showing off (something we know most males, by their very nature, tend to avoid) here are a few ideas that might set you apart from other members of the clan.

- Buy the very best barbecue and tools you can afford. It is a slight pity that everyone else can do too.

- Develop a few favourite recipes of your own and become a master at them. Maybe you've perfected the art of cooking a whole salmon in a kettle barbecue (page 146), or whole eye fillet complete with a crust of red chilli and garlic (page 138–139). It is highly recommended you try these out on family members a number of times before offering them to your competitors – sorry, your mates.

- Tactic number three is to relate yourself to the food. Do this by creating your own special marinade or barbecue sauce and naming it after yourself (mine's called Big Al's Super Sauce). Next time you have the guys around you can reveal your new (insert name here) secret chilli pork baste for all to try. You will then be able to prepare this specialty every time you have a barbecue. It'll become as much a part of your barbecue experience as the tongs and the beer.

If none of these options appeal, there's only one thing for it. Stun other competing males and gain a clear advantage by building your own barbecue! Only then will you have something unique that no one else has – and we all know how good that feels.

Each and every Australian male is equipped with all the necessary skills to build his own backyard barbie; I mean how hard could it be? And what could be better than getting out into the great outdoors and getting down and dirty with a barrow-full of wet cement and a pile of bricks? Don't forget there's also all those manly tools you'll need – like a trowel, a spirit level, a builder's square and a plumb line. Just think: this could be the perfect opportunity to use those overalls you got for Christmas last year that are still crisp, new and sparklingly clean. A man's overalls should always be dirty, after all.

All you have to do now is decide what sort you want to build and where you want to build it. Will it be a simple brick model with a wood fire and a solid grill top, or perhaps you'd like add a small storage space for spare wood and other necessary stuff? Perhaps you'll go further and have a gas grill and plate contraption complete with barbecue tool rack. Or you may decide this is to be the ultimate outdoor cooking machine and have a gas plate, a wood grill and even a wood-fired oven. The choice is yours; the options are endless. Seize the day!

Before you get too carried away, there are a few things to consider before you build your barbecue:

- The first choice to make is the building material. This could be brick, concrete blocks or even natural stone.

- Ensure you build your barbecue in a prominent place. This is to ensure it is a focal point to be seen and envied by every male who visits your home.

- Pick a spot for your barbecue where you can either set a concrete slab or build onto an existing paved area.

- Consider trimming overhanging trees – it's a barbecue we want after all, not a bushfire.

- If it's a brick barbecue you decide on, choose a strong colour brick such as deep orange or red to create the best impression.

- Include space to store fuel and utensils. Also have plenty of flat surfaces around the grill for platters, uncooked food and the all-important beer.

- Ensure you include a few shelves for storage. You could even insert an old sink (complete with drainage) that could be filled with ice to keep drinks cold.

- Then there's a choice of grill or flat plate, or even both if space allows.

- Think big (and about the satisfaction you'll get from your first barbecue of the season).

Now is the time to get you ideas down on paper. If you decide to go for the simplest approach of a brick barbecue with a grill, you can probably get it finished in one Saturday as long as you order everything beforehand.

Once you have decided on where and what you want to build, it's time to visit your local hardware supplier. It's essential you appear knowledgeable so ensure you wear old overalls or shorts, a singlet and work boots. Calling everyone who works at the hardware supplier 'mate' also works a treat, or rely on the time-honoured custom of adding an 'o' or a 'y' at the end of peoples names, such as Johnno and Smithy. Have a list of what you think you need in terms of tools and supplies and describe how big it's to be. Then place an order for everything to be delivered the following Friday afternoon.

For a simple brick and grill barbecue your list should read:

- Small trowel
- Club hammer
- Mason's line
- Spirit level
- String
- Chalk
- Stiff brush
- Mortar mix
- A bag of sand
- Lime
- Bricks 250–300 for a standard barbecue
- Coals tray
- Metal grill and/or plate
- A dozen cold beers (at least)

GETTING STARTED

If you have any trouble with building your very own barbecue, perhaps leave the beer off the shopping list. (Although for some of us this is a crucial part of the ritual – as important as the very bricks and mortar!) You could also build half of it on Saturday, then sit back and view your work for the afternoon over a few cold ones, then resume on Sunday morning.

When it comes to barbecues I'm much more of a buy it, rather than a build it, sort of barbecue guy. Hence the trolley and kettle barbecues in my backyard. But I do have it on very good authority from other barbie builders that these plans work perfectly. If you'd like any more advice there are also excellent instructions at the following websites:

www.rhpeterson.com

www.bbq.netrelief.com

It's worthwhile keeping the telephone number of your local hardware store on hand for any questions, or even a local handyman if you get into serious difficulties.

- Mark up the area of your barbecue with chalk onto your chosen area (either a paved area or a concrete slab poured for this purpose). Remember the size of your grill will dictate the eventual size of your barbecue. The standard height for a barbecue is 12–13 layers of bricks. Open your first beer.

Once you have decided on where and what you want to build, it's time to visit your local hardware supplier. It's essential you appear knowledgeable so ensure you wear old overalls or shorts, a singlet and work boots.

━━ ━━ ━━ ━━ ━━ ━━ ━━ ━━ ━━ ━━ ━━ ━━ ━━ ━━

- The bricklaying design that works well is to lay bricks side by side to make it double thickness. What you want is a double brick wall in a straight-sided U shape with a strong interlocking pattern. Build the base level using this pattern. Begin the second layer with a brick placed sideways in order to make it stronger. You may have to chop a bit off a brick to get the right size. Open your second beer.

- Once you have the hang of the pattern, check the size of this against your grill to ensure it's right. Do not use mortar at this stage to ensure all is well, but remember to leave space between the bricks for the mortar. Open your third beer.

- Make up your mortar mix as directed. For a barbecue, it is recommended to use one part cement to nine parts sand and 1¼ parts lime. This ensures that when the barbecue heats up, it can expand without cracking. Open your fourth beer.

- Apply mortar to the sides of each brick one by one and butt the bricks up against each other. Apply a layer of cement between each layer of bricks. Use a level to make sure that each course is even, and use a builder's square to ensure that the corners come to a perfect 90° angle. Check that the walls are vertical with your plumb line. Complete the first, second and third layers. Open your fifth beer.

- Complete as directed up to the level where the tray will be for coals (it could be about level seven, but feel free to decide yourself). On this level, lay the bricks sideways to produce a small shelf inside the barbecue. Open your sixth beer.

- Build up two more layers, ensuring that each course is even, that the corners are square and the walls are vertical. Then build another level with the bricks sideways to produce a small shelf inside the barbecue for the grill. Open your seventh beer.

- Add another one or two levels to make a wind-break around the grill if preferred.

- Put in your coals tray and cooking grill. Remove any mortar that has squelched out from between the bricks with a stiff brush. Place a layer of bricks on the ground on the inside of the barbecue to complete the job. Open your eighth beer.

- Have an afternoon nap and take the rest of the day off – preferably to drink the remaining beer.

THE POWER OF THE TONGS
AND OTHER SACRED OBJECTS

As every male knows, you need the right tool for the right job. When it comes to barbecuing, this couldn't be truer. Amazingly, many of the best barbecue tools aren't available at barbecue retailers, they're on the shelves of your nearest hardware store. The exception to this rule, of course, is the pair of ever-trusty tongs – the most sacred and intoxicating of all barbecuing implements.

Barbecue tongs

Barbecue tongs have one essential use: to move food around on the grill and barbecue plate. They also have a symbolism that transcends this simple task. Whoever is in charge of the barbecue tongs is in control of the barbecue – indeed, of life as we know it.

Barbecue tongs are the remote control of the backyard. Modern man realised some years ago that incredible power resides with whoever holds them. This is the discerning factor as to why men are so reluctant to give them up.

When choosing barbecue tongs, look for a fairly heavy pair – stainless steel is a good start. Secondly, make sure they're a decent length. This is not to compensate for anything, it's just to get food from the back of the grill without burning your fingers. (Well that's my story and I'm sticking to it. I recommend all male readers of this book do the same.)

Whoever is in charge of the barbecue tongs is in control of the barbecue – indeed, of life as we know it.

▬ ▬ ▬ ▬ ▬ ▬

Spatula/Paint scraper

A spatula is excellent for turning large food items and scraping down a flat-plate after cooking. Ignore the spatulas in barbecue stores – they're totally inadequate. Instead, check out your local hardware store for a wide, triangular paint scraper. These are extremely tough and built to last. (Look for the timber-handled ones and have at least two on hand in various widths.)

Wire brush

A wire brush with strong bristles is required for barbecue cleaning, and again you'll find the best ones in a hardware store. Not only can you usually choose from a couple of different styles and colours (very important for getting in touch with your feminine side), but they're also about 25 per cent cheaper than the barbecue retailers'.

Ignore the spatulas in barbecue stores –
they're just inadequate. Instead, check out
your local hardware store for a wide,
triangular paint scraper. These are
extremely tough and built to last.

It is essential to rack up as many bargains as possible, because the more money you save on equipment, the more money you can spend on beer.

Food brushes

I like to have a few brushes on hand to brush marinades onto meat or a little olive oil onto the grill before cooking. Paint brushes of around 3–4 cm wide are the easiest to use. Some advice: pay for quality. The cheapest ones lose their bristles far too easily.

Skewers

Skewers are indispensable when barbecuing. They can hold tricky ingredients such as prawns flat for cooking and make small ingredients easy to turn and move about on the barbecue. Skewers also provide something to hold onto while eating.

Bamboo skewers must be soaked in cold water for at least an hour before use to ensure they don't burn. The bonus, though, is that there's no washing up.

Metal skewers are my all time favourite as they never

burn like timber ones can. Purchase flat, long bladed skewers, rather than round skewers. This way the ingredients won't spin around on the skewer as you try to turn them. Rosemary branches, sugar cane, or lemongrass stalks can also be used as skewers. They're ideal, as they add flavour and don't burn so easily either.

Matches

Matches are essential for obvious reasons – especially if you're a devotee of kettle or open-fire barbecues. Unfortunately, there comes a time in every trolley barbecue's life when the automatic ignition packs it in and you'll need to manually kick-start her. Use extra long matches to prevent burnt fingers.

The barbecue apron

While I don't usually like to comment on other bloke's clothes, I'll make an exception here. The barbecue apron is an essential item of clothing for any serious barbecue cook. Few dedicated barbecuers would be seen without one: do you really want to wear the fat that splatters off the grill?

Rosemary branches, sugar cane, or lemongrass stalks can also be used as skewers. They're ideal, as they add flavour and don't burn so easily either.

▬ ▬ ▬ ▬ ▬ ▬ ▬ ▬ ▬ ▬ ▬ ▬ ▬

There are two main styles of apron available to the barbecue cook in Australia today: traditional and humorous.

Traditional barbecue aprons are available as off-the-shelf designs and usually only come in classic black. These aprons are considered to be fully run-in when completely stained with the remains of past barbecue meals. They are rarely washed. More commonly worn by trendy inner-city types.

Alternatively, there's the humorous apron – and the more tasteless they are the better. They're typically emblazoned with crude jokes at the expense of women, children and small animals. Some sport their own pair of plastic breasts, among other appendages. More commonly worn by your outer-suburban bloke.

In recent times, barbecue fashion has extended beyond the humble apron. For many hosts nowa-days, surf shirts and Hawaiian prints are essential. Shorts are also a must: knee-length and accessorised with a wide brim straw hat and a heavy coating of zinc on the nose.

THE SECRET'S IN THE SIZZLE

'Fire is your friend'

New York chef Mario Batali

Whether you cook on a trolley barbecue, a kettle barbecue or over an open fire, it's the fire that's often the key to good barbecuing. But be warned: this is not a subject to be taken lightly as fire is one of the magic ingredients that draws men to this primeval experience in the first place.

Fire is the commencement of the barbecuing process – unless, of course, you stalk and kill your own wild animals. That's why those of us who hunt at the local butcher love the fire bit. This may also be the reason why we compensate with *really* big barbecue equipment, but let's leave the speculation out of it.

A good way to manage heat is to have one part of your barbecue at a slightly lower temperature than the rest. This will give you somewhere to put food that is cooking too quickly.

It's also important you keep your barbecue clean – especially if you want your pride and joy to last for more than one summer. Worse still, imagine if it caught fire while your mates are watching you demonstrate your skill of the grill.

FIRING UP A GAS BARBIE

One of the keys to good gas barbecuing is to ensure you cook over an even heat source. All you have to do to prepare is light it, turn the gas to high under the section you want to cook on and allow it to heat for 10–15 minutes. Then, reduce the heat to the desired temperature (ideal is around medium–high) just before you're ready to cook.

If you're cooking over a grill, your barbecue may have a layer of heat-retaining rocks (sometimes called lava rocks or ceramic rocks). These rocks stop gas flames reaching the food, store heat and radiate it upward to create a hot surface over which to cook. Ensure they are spread evenly so they conduct the heat properly. Over time, lava rocks soak up fat and cease to conduct heat effectively, so they'll need to be replaced from time to time.

Ceramic rocks (which require a grid to sit on) prevent flare-ups, last even longer than lava rocks, and provide a more even heat. Ceramic rocks are a worthwhile investment if you use your barbecue extensively. The only downside is that they take a little longer to heat up than lava rocks.

A good way to manage heat is to have one part of your barbecue at a slightly lower temperature than the rest. This will give you somewhere to put food that is cooking too quickly. Alternatively, have one really hot spot for searing steaks and the like quickly, then move them to cook over the medium–high part of the grill.

Once your barbecue is hot, simply brush a thin layer of olive oil onto the barbecue plate or grill before you're about to cook. This will prevent food sticking. Olive oil on a piece of kitchen paper or a brush will do the trick.

CLEANING UP A GAS BARBIE

After cooking, raise the gas to high for 3–4 minutes. Scour the grill with a wire brush to remove any remaining fat and food scraps. While the barbecue plate is hot, remove food scraps with a triangle scraper and wipe over with absorbent paper. When the barbecue is completely cold, brush the plate and grill with cooking oil and cover until next required. Don't forget: turn the gas off.

FIRING UP A KETTLE BARBIE

As with all barbecuing, the trick is in the fire. Light your kettle barbecue in a spot out of the wind. You'll need to pay close attention during the early stages to ensure a proper cooking temperature is reached.

You can either cook directly over a bed of coals or build a fire that works on indirect heat. This is done by making a stack of glowing coals on either side of the barbecue. The fuel for a kettle barbecue is typically coal-based and the beads of fuel must be heated until they've got a coating of white ash on them.

To get your barbecue to this stage, stack about a kilogram of beads on opposites sides of the barbecue, leaning them up against the metal sides. Divide six firelighters between each stack. Light the firelighters and keep watch to ensure they flame well. You may need to fan the fire a little to keep it going at a good speed. Two kilograms of fuel (one kilogram on each side of the barbie) will provide about two hours cooking time, so add more at the beginning if you plan to cook for a longer period. There are now instant brands of fuel that don't require firelighters, so check the packet instructions.

When the white ash stage is reached, place the lid on the barbecue and open the top and bottom vents. The barbecue is now hot and ready to use.

Insert the upper cooking rack and place food to be cooked on upper rack in the centre of the kettle barbecue. Cover with the lid to create an oven effect.

For direct cooking, spread the glowing coals out over the bottom rack and insert the upper cooking rack. Brush a thin layer of olive oil onto the barbecue grill before adding food. This will stop food sticking. Olive oil on a piece of kitchen paper or a brush will do the trick.

CLEANING UP A KETTLE BARBIE

Kettle barbecues need to be completely cooled before cleaning. Sweep all the ash into the bottom tray and discard. Remove wire racks and gently scrub them clean with a wire brush. Wash the inside of the barbecue with cold water and dry it with newspaper. Do the same for the outside of the barbecue. Put barbecue back together and cover until next required. The cold ash is excellent on the garden.

FIRING UP AN OPEN-FIRE BARBIE

To prepare an open fire you'll need paper, kindling (such as small sticks), larger sticks and split logs or charcoal.

To fire your barbecue, place twists of newspaper and kindling underneath the cooking grill. Light them and allow the fire to catch. Gradually add twigs, small sticks and then larger sticks as the fire takes hold. Lastly, add logs and allow to burn down to red embers – this will take 1–2 hours. Experience will dictate the amount of logs needed. Once you have red embers, there is little you can do to adjust the heat they produce. Avoid cooking over roaring flames as this will blacken and burn your food.

To prepare a charcoal fire follow the directions as above, but add charcoal in place of the split logs. Alternatively, use firelighters beneath charcoal as described in kettle barbecues. Charcoal is ready to cook over once it is covered with white ash.

Brush a thin layer of olive oil onto the barbecue grill before adding food. This prevents food from sticking. Olive oil on a piece of kitchen paper or a brush will do the trick. Watch carefully when using a fire (before, during and after cooking), to ensure it doesn't get out of control, and that children are kept at a safe distance. You can also try wrapping potatoes, onions and other vegetables in foil and cooking them in the red embers. This source of heat is also ideal for toasting marshmallows.

CLEANING UP AN OPEN-FIRE BARBIE

Allow the fire to cool completely before scraping out the ash and dead embers. Cold ash is excellent on the garden beds. Clean the grill or plate with a wire brush. Brush with oil before leaving for your next barbecue feast.

Now that you've decided on the type of barbecue, you're just about ready to start sizzling!

THE BARBECUE COOK'S PANTRY

Having the right equipment for the job doesn't just mean having a great pair of barbecue tongs and a full gas bottle – it also means having the right ingredients on hand to cook with. This includes everything from olive oil and spices to specific cuts of meat and even certain types of salt.

This is my ultimate beginner's guide to choosing the right ingredients for success at the barbecue.

Banana leaves

Perfect for wrapping whole fish in before barbecuing. You should find them at you local Asian grocer but if not, aluminium foil is a good substitute.

Beef

All manner of beef cuts are used for barbecuing. Steak include eye fillet, porterhouse, rib, rump, scotch and T-bone. Other useful cuts include beef ribs and minced beef.

Black beans

Fermented, salted black beans are used to make black bean sauce, among other Asian marinades. It's a good idea to soak them in cold water before use to remove excess salt.

Bok choy

A green, leafy Asian vegetable. Very small ones are tender enough to be used as the base of a salad.

Burghal

Commonly used in tabouli, burghal is also ideal for adding a crunchy coating to lamb kofta burgers.

Breadcrumbs

Readily available in supermarkets, breadcrumbs are essential for making burgers and meatballs.

Butter

Good quality butter is indispensable for the barbie cook. Brush over pineapple as it cooks on the grill. Oddly enough, it is also a fundamental ingredient in garlic butter.

Chicken

Virtually every cut of chicken can be used on the barbecue – chicken fillets, chops, drumsticks, wings and even chicken mince. A whole chicken is also easy to barbecue.

Chickpeas

Chickpeas are ideal in salads and veggie burgers. They are readily available dried (in which case they need to be soaked in cold water overnight, then boiled until tender). They can also be purchased ready-cooked in cans.

Chillies

Fresh chillies are frequently used when barbecuing, especially for marinades and basting sauces. They are available as either green or red. Take care to remove the seeds and membrane from inside a chilli before you chop it, as this is where the intense burning heat is.

Chilli paste, commonly called sambal oelek in Asian grocers, is also very good with barbecued food. Adjust the amount you use to suite your tastes.

Sweet chilli sauce is widely available. As the name suggests, it is sweet and mild.

Coconut milk and cream

Made from grated coconut soaked in hot water, coconut milk and coconut cream are ideal in a variety of marinades and basting sauces. Coconut milk is lighter and thinner than coconut cream; both are readily available in cans from supermarkets.

Curry paste

Curry pastes, such as tandoori and Thai, are very handy in marinades when you want to add a hot burst of flavour to food.

Duck

Duck is not as popular as other poultry, but it is excellent on the barbecue. Duck fillets are great to cook, as is whole duck.

Feta

Feta cheese is a firm, white, slightly salty cheese and is widely available in supermarkets and delicatessens. It is an essential ingredient of Greek salad.

Fish

Fish can be tricky to cook on the barbecue but with the right training, anyone can do it. Firm varieties, such as ocean trout, salmon cutlets and fillets, sardines, tuna, blue eye and flathead, are best suited to barbecuing.

Fish sauce

A tangy thin sauce made from salted fish – essential in many Asian dishes. Perfect for adding a salty flavour burst to food.

Garlic

Garlic is an essential component in all types of

cooking, and barbecuing is no exception. It is vital in marinades, spice mixes, chutneys and sauces. Garlic powder is also available as a substitute.

Gelatine

Gelatine is used to set desserts. It comes in a powdered and a sheet form and is available in delicatessens and food stores. Sheet gelatine is considerably better tasting than powdered gelatine.

Ginger

Ginger is readily available at all fruit and vegetable shops. It needs to be peeled then grated before being used in burger mixes, marinades and relishes.

Harissa

From Tunisia in North Africa, harissa is a fiery chilli paste with a smoky flavour. Chilli paste may be used as a substitute.

Herbs

Herbs are essential for adding a fresh burst of flavour to burger mixes, sauces and salsas, salads and marinades. In this book you'll come across basil leaves, coriander leaves, curly parsley, flat leaf parsley, thyme, mint and rosemary. Dried herbs such as thyme and oregano are a good substitute if no fresh herbs are available.

Italian sponge finger biscuits

Known to Italians as savoiardi, Italian sponge fingers are available in supermarkets and are a main ingredient in tiramisu.

Kecap manis

Kecap manis is a thick, sweet Indonesian soy sauce. It is ideal for adding a sweet soy flavour to marinades and basting mixes and is widely available at Asian grocery stores and larger supermarkets.

Lamb

Lamb is the wonder meat of the Australian barbecue. You can cook fillets, lamb loin chops, lamb mince, leg of lamb, cutlets and even spit roast a whole lamb.

Lemons

Use lemon juice or zest to add freshness to your cooking. Lemon wedges can also be served with barbecued seafood.

Limes

Limes are used in much the same way as lemons, just with a sharper flavour. Lime wedges are brilliant served with barbecued prawns.

Mascarpone

Mascarpone is a fresh Italian cheese with a rich sour cream flavour. It is essential when making tiramisu.

Mayonnaise

Mayonnaise is an essential sauce for the barbecue table. Ensure you buy a well made one that is neither too sweet nor too runny. Beef up your mayonnaise by adding a little lemon or lime juice to it.

Mirin

Mirin is sweetened Japanese sake that is available in Asian grocers. It adds a shine and sweetness to Japanese barbecue glazes and basting sauces.

Mustard

Mustard is essential for serving with barbecued steaks, chops and cutlets. It can also be used to add great flavour to marinades. Have both smooth and seeded mustard on hand.

Olive oil

Olive oil is a must at all barbecues. Brush onto the barbecue before cooking; use it to make marinades, salad dressings and countless other things. You should use a pure olive oil for brushing onto the barbecue and an extra virgin olive oil for all other uses.

Prawns

Prawns make fantastic kebabs on the barbecue. Ensure you purchase green prawns, which are still raw. They should have their shell peeled off before cooking.

Prosciutto

Prosciutto, also known as parma ham, is a salted air-dried ham that is excellent wrapped around chicken kebabs to add a salty-bacon flavour.

Pork

Pork gives us so much to enjoy on the barbecue. From sausages and pork ribs to pork mince, fillet, neck, ribs, loin and leg.

Salt

Salt is an essential flavour enhancer when barbecuing. I use sea salt, as it has a finer mineral flavour than common table salt.

Sesame oil

Sesame oil is a rich aromatic oil made from roasted sesame seeds. Only a small amount is needed to add flavour to dressings and marinades.

Spices

Spices are evident on virtually every page of this book. In fact, I'm not sure what I would do without them. The following spices should be in your store cupboard in order to deal with every barbecue emergency.

Black pepper, white pepper, allspice, cardamom, cayenne pepper, cinnamon, coriander seeds, cumin seeds, five-spice, nutmeg, oregano, Sichuan pepper, star anise, sweet paprika and turmeric.

Soy sauce

Soy sauce is an essential ingredient when making Asian marinades, sauces and dressings.

Tabasco

Tabasco sauce is a fiery American chilli sauce that is great for bringing a burst of heat to barbecued food.

Vanilla extract

Vanilla extract is a pure extraction of crushed vanilla pods, producing a thick aromatic liquid. It is essential for pavlova and other barbecue-friendly desserts.

Vegetables

Vegetables are perfect for adding different colours, textures and flavours to the usual barbecued offerings. Many different vegetables are used in salads, on kebabs and to make vegetarian foods. The following are regularly used in this book: beetroot, capsicum, cos lettuce, corn, cucumbers, eggplant, green beans, mushrooms, onions and zucchini.

Vinegar

Vinegar is the essential ingredient, along with olive oil, in salad dressing. It is therefore mandatory to have a couple of good ones on hand. Visit a good delicatessen and search for a sherry, a red wine and a balsamic vinegar.

WORKING UP A THIRST

BARBECUES AND BEER

There's no doubt that beer is the number one beverage at all Australian barbecues. In fact, it's virtually mandatory for the blokes to enjoy a cooling ale or two as they gather around the barbecue and comment on the skill – or otherwise – of the host. A slab, or in some cases a keg, is as much a part of the ritual and ceremony for some men as the food itself.

Accordingly, if beer is the drink of choice there has to be lots of ice too. Depending on the size of the gathering, you may well need two or three eskies full of the stuff. In most Australian backyards, there's usually a back shed with an old fridge well-stocked with Dad's favourite beer, which is very handy for barbecue gatherings.

Stubby holders are another 'must-have' barbecue item. They keep your beer at an appropriate drinking temperature, and you probably won't need glasses for the beer drinkers either.

It's always a good idea to set aside one tub of ice for a few bottles of soft drink: the littlies need something to drink too, as well as the unlucky designated drivers.

One of the traditional uses for beer at a barbecue was to pour a little of it over the meat while cooking. For the sake of beer and culinary evolution, forget that your father has done it all his life, and passed this little gem of information onto you. It does absolutely nothing whatsoever for the meat. All you are doing is wasting precious alcohol.

Despite the fact that beer is a universally loved drink, it's important to bring something other than VB. Lager is the usual starting point for most blokes, with choices ranging from special brew to ice brew and everything else in between. Don't forget: there's a whole world of beer out there, so go out and try it!

At your next barbecue, expand your horizons and rock up with some Irish stout or a few bottles of Belgian Trappist monks', beer. British beers are also fairly widely available nowadays, so you could seek out some traditional English or Scottish ales. German wheat beers are also good for making an impression. The beer options are endless,

One of the traditional uses for beer at a barbecue was to pour a little of it over the meat while cooking. Forget it! All you are doing is wasting precious alcohol.

extending from Mexico to China; the USA to Luxembourg.

If you're really keen, brew your own in the back shed – just make sure you taste a bottle or two at home before offering it to anyone else.

BARBECUES AND WINE

Wine is increasingly making its presence felt at Aussie barbecues these days. In order for the modern male to appear sophisticated, you'll need to be up to date on the whole wine thing. Pop down to the local bottle shop and you'll be surrounded by more bottles of the stuff than you can poke a stick at. So where do you start?

Wine is labelled in three ways. Where the wine comes from; the type of grape used; and the year it was made. It's as simple as that. The white wine options list below gives some idea of they they'll taste like.

If you're in charge of the tongs you shouldn't drink too much before showing off your skill of the grill. There'll be plenty of time to catch up when you've packed the tongs away.

Don't bother reading the back label too much: it's usually just the wine maker waffling on about how the wine was made and the weather conditions the grapes grew in –

as if you care! Instead look for a wine that fits the budget. Generally, new release wines are cheaper than older wines.

No matter what drinks you choose to serve at your barbecue, always remember that if you're in charge of the tongs you shouldn't drink too much before showing off your skill of the grill. There'll be plenty of time to catch up when you've packed the tongs away.

WHITE WINE OPTIONS

White wine is usually served in the early stages of a barbie, just to get things started you know, before the real drinking begins. If you're having a seafood barbecue, you may wish to stick with white wine all the way through.

Sparkling white wine

It's fairly common these days to pop the cork on a bottle or two of sparkling wine, or champagne as it's often called, as guests arrive. Sparkling wine is white wine with bubbles in it – the strange thing is that it doesn't taste of much at all: just lots of fizz and fun in a bottle.

Riesling

Riesling tends to be packed with lemon and lime flavours and is typically crisp and dry. It's usually one of the cheaper wines available, and it's best to buy the year's current release. Good to have if you're enjoying a few fishy nibbles before the main food.

Chardonnay

Chardonnay is a perennial favourite at Australian backyards dos. It suits all types of meats from chicken and turkey to fish and prawns. You'll find chardonnay in all price brackets, so choose one that fits yours.

Semillon

Semillon is my least favourite white wine but for the sake of equality, I have included it here. As a young wine, it has masses of juicy lemon flavours and a slightly spicy tingle on the tongue. It's probably a good wine for the novice drinker to begin with, as the taste is quite bland and subtle.

Sauvignon blanc

In comparison to semillon, sauvignon blanc is at the opposite end of the flavour spectrum. Instead of subtlety, it's jam packed with flavours like lemons, limes, gooseberries and an amazing crispy finish. Best served quite cool.

Semillon-Sauvignon blanc

This blend brings together two very different attributes. The semillon tames the crisp lemon and lime acidity of the sauvignon blanc to produce what many (me included) consider the perfect summer drink.

Pinot gris

This is a relative newcomer on the Australian market. It's a white wine that is perfect with seafood. It is rich and crisp in the mouth and has subtle flavours including spices, honey and summer fruits. Well worth a try.

RED WINE OPTIONS

Red wine is a much more manly drink, and in choosing which wine you're to offer, most guys stick to the old mantra of bigger is better. For example a big, gutsy bottle of red wine – the sort of thing that puts hairs on your chest – is obviously going to be better than some wussy little number.

This may seem over the top but don't forget the wine will have to compete with gutsy barbecued food and the wafting aromatic smoke on a hot sunny day. So subtle wines probably won't stand much of a chance.

Try to get your hands on a magnum of red. These are bottles that contain 1.5 litres of wine – twice the size of a regular bottle. The impression that something of this magnitude can make at a barbecue is not to be underestimated. If it's twice as big as regular bottles it's sure to be twice as good as anyone else's wine!

Sparkling red wine

Yes, you can buy red wine with bubbles (in fact, some would say it's an Australian wine icon), and it tends to be a great fit at any barbecue. It's very good (very,

very good in fact) with barbecued duck, quail, turkey, beef and lamb.

Cabernet

Cabernet – now there's a strong name if ever I heard one. It possesses good medium-strength blackcurrant and chocolate flavours and a decent whack of tannin, making it well suited to anything beefy such as steak, ribs and burgers. This is one of the most popular wines at Aussie barbecues.

Shiraz

Shiraz follows a very close second to cabernet in the Australian barbecue popularity stakes. It tends to be a bit bigger, fuller and richer with a hint of sweetness and spice in the wine. This means it matches well with meats that have been cooked with a spicy marinade. It's also perfect with big, fat barbecued pork sausages.

Grenache

Grenache is a great wine to ease yourself into the whole red wine caper. It's relatively inexpensive, packed with easy to drink raspberry and stewed plum flavours and offers a decent whack of spicy flavours. Well worth a run at your next barbecue.

Merlot

Merlot is a wine for those who like big flavours, which can be important at a barbecue to match up to the food. It typically has very appealing blackcurrant, rhubarb and fruitcake flavours, with a hint of tannin and a slight sweetness.

Pinot noir

Pinot noir is a very special wine because, at its best, it has a wonderful velvety texture and unmistakable gamey, mushroomy, plum and berry flavours. The only problem with pinot is that these subtle characteristics can easily be lost in the heat and flavour of a typical barbecue.

Rosé

Rosé is a light, translucent red wine – more pink than red. The reason it's pink is because the wine doesn't stay in contact with the grape skins very long and therefore doesn't get much of a colour. Despite its pale colour, rosé has good flavours of cherries, berries and subtle spice and is well matched with salmon, turkey, prawns and spicy chicken. Best served chilled.

Part 2

THE GRILL

BARBECUE GOLDEN RULES

The essential rules to keep you – and your barbecue – on the right track.

Once you've chosen the right barbecue – be it a trolley, kettle or open-fire barbecue – you need the right tools for the job.

First up, you need barbecue tongs, a spatula/paint scraper, a wire brush, a couple of good food brushes, packets of skewers and a barbecue apron.

Fire

A good fire is your best friend when preparing barbecued food. Get it right and you're halfway to barbecue glory.

Keep it clean

It's essential to keep your barbecue clean. Clean up properly every time you cook.

The right ingredients

Don't be half-arsed about your ingredients. Spend a little extra to get the right stuff and you'll be well on the way to creating great tasting food.

Setting up

Have everything on hand *before* you start cooking. This is not only efficient, it ensures you can pay attention to your cooking and drink uninterrupted.

Don't flip

Leave the food alone! Let it cook to perfection on one side before turning it over. Your taste buds will thank you for it.

Spicing it up

The fine art of using spices guarantees a lifetime of enjoyable barbecue eating.

Sausage sizzle

Don't ever prick holes in your sausages. All this does is let the fat and the flavours leak out.

Don't be afraid of bones

Practice cooking fish and meat on the bone and you'll be rewarded with moist, juicy food.

Meat on a stick

Learn the knack of cooking kebabs and you'll never look back.

Grill marks

Cooking the perfect steak makes you an absolute bloody legend.

Don't give up smoking

Learn how to hot smoke a whole salmon and you'll never go hungry again.

Cooking over coals

Perfect spit roasting and you'll be totally in touch with your inner prehistoric man.

Cool salads

Always balance out your meat offerings with plenty of cool salads.

THE SKILL OF THE GRILL

SETTING UP

The big barbecue day has finally arrived. You're prepared and rigorously trained; you've been practicing your flipping motion in the backyard; tried your apron on for size and been down to the barbecue shop several times for extra supplies. You've played around with the fire and now it's time to get sizzling.

Start cooking when – and only when – you've got everything you might need at your fingertips. Wandering off to the kitchen every few minutes to get another handful of skewers or to refill the olive oil bottle while food is on the grill is not recommended. As Murphy's Law dictates, this is the time that flare-ups will most likely occur.

Start cooking when – and only when – you've got everything you might need at your fingertips. As Murphy's Law dictates, this is the time that flare-ups will most likely occur.

Depending on what you're planning to cook, some of the items you'll need are: olive oil, salt and pepper, fresh herbs, spice mixes, marinades and aluminium foil. You'll also need utensils: tongs, a spatula, brushes, skewers, wire brush, matches and a barbecue apron. Don't forget: clean platters or plates for the food once it's cooked too.

One of the challenges that every barbecue cook faces is the inevitable total fire ban day. The rule in most states around Australia now mean that only barbecues classified as 'controlled barbecues' can be lit on total fire ban days. This means electric barbecues or gas barbecues where the heat can be easily extinguished.

- Barbecues that use solid fuel such as wood, charcoal or briquettes are banned. This includes closed oven or kettle-type appliances.

- It always pays to have a connected water hose nearby, in case of an emergency. Alternatively, have at least ten litres of water on hand.

- An area of three metres around and above the barbecue should be completely cleared of all flammable material.

- A responsible person should be in attendance at all times.

Safe food handling is another issue you should be up-to-date with. Here are a few basic food-handling tips that all barbie cooks should follow in order to ensure your food is hygienic to eat.

- Don't get the meat out of the fridge until you're read to cook it.

- Ensure meat is cooked correctly. Pork (including sausages) and chicken must be cooked until no pink remains.

- Never leave meat to sit in the full sun before cooking.

- Never put cooked meat back onto a platter that has had raw meat on it, as any bacteria from the raw food juices will be transferred to the cooked meat.

CHOOSING YOUR PREY

Number one enemy of the barbecue is excess fat. Fat likes nothing more than to flare-up, catch alight, burn the food and occasionally you. Flare-ups blacken the food and cause carcinogenic crusts and unpleasant tastes. Putting heavily marinated food onto the barbecue without draining it can also cause flare-ups. Choose trim meat and keep a close eye on food as it cooks.

BIG LESSON

It's time to face your worst fears. Flipping, flopping, tossing and turning meat around the grill is a real no-no: you're not giving your food a chance to cook

Flipping, flopping, tossing and turning meat around the grill is a real no-no: you're not giving your food a chance to cook properly.

━ ━ ━ ━ ━ ━ ━

properly. Take my word for it, you don't want some savvy sheila coming up and telling you how to do it properly. Worse still, imagine if she took the tongs off you and showed you how it should be done. You should really only have to turn meat over once.

SERVING UP

I love the casual food feel of a barbecue: everyone's outdoors, the sun is shining (hopefully), the children are running around and everybody's relaxing. In order to maintain this theme, it's best to serve up all your barbecued food on large platters. This way everyone can pick and choose. Moreover, your guests won't leave any behind when they only take what they want to eat.

SPICE MIXES, MARINADES AND BASTES

The art of using spice mixes, marinades and bastes is one that many young barbecue cooks fail to learn. They're too busy rushing off to cook T-bone steaks, lamb chops and pork spare ribs. This is a great pity because if they take the time to learn the most basic combinations, they'll have a barbecue skill that will last a lifetime.

Just imagine the aromas that will come from cooking prawn kebabs that have been marinated in soy sauce, ginger and chilli, and the mouth watering flavours that come from marinating a whole chicken in a magical North African spice mix of ground coriander, cumin, sweet paprika and lemon juice.

The actual making and use of spice mixes, marinades and bastes is incredibly easy – child's play, in fact.

The actual making and use of spice mixes, marinades and bastes is incredibly easy – child's play, in fact. All you need to do is brush them onto your meat just before you want to cook. If time is short, you can even apply them to food that is already on the grill. There are even recipes here which are spooned over meat after it has been cooked.

With marinades, it's important to drain them well before barbecuing. Otherwise, the marinade will drip and cause flare-ups – blackening your food and making it taste really unpleasant. Small amounts of marinade may be brushed lightly onto food as it cooks. With large pieces of meat, it's best to leave them to marinate overnight.

The following recipes offer a great cross section of my favourite spice mixes and marinades, so feel free to mix and match them as wish. In fact, this is an area where it's easy to come up with your own *secret* blend with which to wow your fellow barbecuing mates.

Just think: with a little practice, you'll soon be infusing your barbecue cooking with the aromas and flavourings of the world's cuisines.

NEW ORLEANS CAJUN SPICE RUB

Cajun cooking hails from New Orleans in the USA. It's incredibly tasty: hot and spicy. This recipe is fantastic on fish and chicken.

1 tbsp sweet paprika

1 tbsp garlic powder

2 tsp ground oregano

1 tsp white pepper

1 tbsp onion powder

2 tsp ground thyme

1 tsp cayenne pepper

1 tsp freshly ground black pepper

> Mix the ingredients together and sprinkle onto food before barbecuing.

NORTH AFRICAN SPICE MIX

The spicy flavours of North Africa typically include coriander, cumin, sweet paprika, lemon juice and olive oil. This combination is particularly good on lamb, beef and quail.

1 tsp ground coriander

1 tsp sweet paprika

1½ tbsp lemon juice

1 tsp ground cumin

½ tsp salt

2 tbsp olive oil

> Mix all of the ingredients together to form a smooth paste. Brush onto food before barbecuing or as it's cooking.

CHERMOULA SPICE MIX

Chermoula is a classic spice blend that hails from North Africa. This spice mix is perfectly suited to seafood, and I love it on things like prawn kebabs and salmon fillets.

2 tsp sweet paprika
1 tsp chilli powder
1 tsp ground coriander
½ tsp ground cardamom
½ tsp allspice
2 tbsp lemon juice

1 tsp ground ginger
1 tsp ground cumin
1 tsp ground white pepper
½ tsp ground cinnamon
1 tsp salt
3 tbsp olive oil

> Mix all of the ingredients together to form a smooth paste. Brush onto food before barbecuing or as it's cooking.

CHINESE SALT AND PEPPER SPICE

This easy-to-make mix comes from the Sichuan region of China and is usually served alongside crispy skinned chicken. Try it yourself on quail and chicken kebabs or sprinkled onto lamb cutlets.

3 tsp Sichuan pepper
½ tsp five-spice

½ tsp salt

> Place the salt and pepper in a dry pan and cook over medium heat. Stir until the salt turns a sandy brown colour, usually about 3–4 minutes. Crush until very fine in a mortar and pestle. Sieve pepper to remove husks and stir the five-spice through.

> Mix the ingredients together and sprinkle onto food before barbecuing or as it's cooking.

TEXAN BARBECUE BASTE

This is an old-style baste that is perfect on full-flavoured meats such as beef, kangaroo and duck. Be warned: it has quite a kick!

4 tbsp tomato sauce	1 tbsp Worcestershire sauce
1 tbsp white vinegar	1 tbsp brown sugar
2 tsp mustard	1 tsp chilli powder
1/2 tsp salt	1/4 tsp Tabasco

> Combine ingredients in a saucepan and bring to the boil. Reduce to a simmer and cook for 5 minutes. Allow to cool then use as a marinade or brush onto meat as it's barbecuing to create a delicious coating.

GUTSY BLACK BEAN AND CHILLI MARINADE

This Chinese-inspired mix of black beans and chilli is especially good on chicken kebabs and pork spare ribs.

1 tbsp black beans, soaked in cold water for
    10 minutes, then drained
2 tbsp soy sauce
1 tbsp fish sauce
2 tsp chilli paste or sauce
1 tsp sesame oil
2 tsp grated ginger

> Mash black beans with a fork then add remaining ingredients. Brush this onto meat before barbecuing or as it's cooking.

INDIAN TANDOORI MARINADE

The subtle flavour of tandoori is famous around the world. It's at its best on chicken fillets, lamb fillets and lamb cutlets.

4 tbsp natural yoghurt
2 tbsp tandoori paste
1 tbsp lemon juice

> Whisk the ingredients together to form a smooth paste. Brush onto meat before barbecuing or as it's cooking.

ALL-TIME FAVOURITE TEXAN BASTE

This one really packs a punch and my favourite ways of using it are on chicken wings, chicken drumsticks and beef ribs.

1 garlic clove, crushed
1 tsp chilli powder
1 tsp sweet paprika
1 tsp mustard
½ tsp ground coriander
½ tsp ground cumin
½ tsp freshly ground black pepper
½ tsp salt
2 tbsp olive oil

> Mix the ingredients together and brush onto meat before barbecuing or as it's cooking.

ORIENTAL SOY AND GARLIC MARINADE

This is an effortless marinade that works wonders on chicken, fish and pork.

2 tbsp white vinegar
2 tbsp soy sauce
1 garlic clove, crushed
1 tsp caster sugar
Pinch of five-spice
A few drops of Tabasco

> Whisk all the ingredients together and brush onto meat before barbecuing or as it's cooking.

CARIBBEAN FRESH LIME MARINADE

This is brilliant when you're looking for something a little different to the usual run-of-the-mill flavours. It's excellent spooned over fish after cooking.

3 tbsp lime juice
¼ cup finely sliced spring onions
1 small red chilli, de-seeded and finely diced
½ tsp salt
Large pinch of allspice
2 tbsp olive oil

> Mix all ingredients together and spoon onto food after barbecuing.

LIP-SMACKING LIME AND CHILLI MARINADE

This is a family favourite at our place, and the children don't even seem to notice the fact that there's chilli in it. Exceptional on chicken wings and lamb cutlets.

3 tbsp lime juice
1 small red chilli, de-seeded and finely diced
1 tsp caster sugar
½ tsp salt
2 tbsp olive oil

> Whisk all the ingredients together and brush onto meat. Allow to marinate for 30 minutes before barbecuing. Drain off excess marinade and use to baste meat during cooking.

THAI COCONUT CURRY BASTE

This is the perfect way to add a mild curry flavour to barbecued food without overpowering it. It is especially good with prawns, fish kebabs and chicken.

2 tbsp red Thai curry paste
200 ml (7 fl oz) coconut cream

> Place curry paste and coconut cream in a small saucepan. Bring to the boil and simmer for a couple of minutes. Add salt to taste. Brush the cooled marinade onto food as it cooks on the barbecue.

COOKING SAUSAGES AND BURGERS

Sausages and burgers are the perfect way for the L-plater barbecue chef to hone his skills. By cooking these two simple foods, you'll soon be master of the tongs; moving the food around the grill correctly and having everything cooked to perfection at the same time. All of these skills take time to conquer and it's important that these are accomplished properly before moving onto bigger and better things.

Sausages are a staple food of most barbecues. Don't skimp: always buy good quality sausage. Forget the family pack at the supermarket meat department, the Saturday specials at your local market, or 'barbecue' packs from dubious butchers. These tend to be made with heaps of fat and cereal fillers – boring stuff to the barbecue connoisseur.

> *Sausages and burgers are the perfect way for the L-plater barbecue chef to hone his skills.*

Instead, head down to your local European butcher

and choose from his bratwurst range. Bratwurst sausages are typically made with a mixture of coarsely ground pork and beef and are seasoned to perfection. They cook beautifully on the barbecue and are succulent, tasty and juicy to eat.

The are a couple of golden rules to remember when cooking sausages:

- Never, ever prick holes in them before or during cooking. All this does is let the fat escape and cause flames to roar up from your coals. It's the fat that provides the juiciness in a sausage, so you'll want to keep it inside.

- Have a part of your barbecue at medium heat so your sausages can cook gently if required. Really thick sausages can be pre-cooked in a pot of boiling water for 2–3 minutes. Drain and cool them quickly. This will prevent them splitting open on the barbecue.

- Last but not least, never serve a burnt sausage.

Burgers are brilliant because virtually everyone, young and old, loves them. Most butchers offer a great range of different minced meats aside from beef: there should be pork, chicken, lamb and maybe even veal. If not, most butchers are only too happy to oblige and mince some for you on the spot. Don't purchase 'diet' mince because it's too low in fat. You need some fat to keep the burger juicy.

The expertise needed for burgers is fairly straightforward. Burgers cook quicker on a flat plate because there is more surface heat, but it's the grill where you can be clever and add the authentic grill marks.

Sausages are a staple food of most barbecues. Forget the family pack at the supermarket ... these tend to be made with heaps of fat and cereal fillers – boring stuff to the barbecue connoisseur.

AUSSIE CEVAPCICI

Cevapcici are a traditional skinless sausage from the Balkan region of South-eastern Europe. They look more like a burger than a sausage and are rectangular-shaped. You can vary the flavours to suit your tastes by adding more chilli, some spices or fresh herbs. Thanks for the recipe Jonathan.

500 g (1 lb) minced beef
500 g (1 lb) minced pork
1 tsp salt
¼ tsp ground white pepper
½ tsp freshly ground black pepper
1 garlic clove, crushed
Large pinch of chilli powder

> Mix all the ingredients together really well then divide mix into 20 x 50g (1¾ oz) portions. Pat them into thin, rectangular shapes and flatten slightly.

> Cook the cevapcici on a hot barbecue for around 10 minutes, turning 3–4 times. Serve with crusty bread and a dollop of a spicy tomato relish.

Makes 20 burgers.

BEEF BURGERS

A perfectly cooked beef burger is a joy to behold: full flavoured, juicy and delicious. Do it right with all the trimmings: bacon, egg, lettuce, beetroot and your own homemade barbecue sauce (page 177) and you'll be considered an absolute legend.

1 kg (2 lb) beef mince
1 small onion, diced
2 tbsp tomato paste or tomato sauce
Salt and freshly ground black pepper

> Mix all the ingredients together. Divide into 10 and form into burger shapes.

> Place burgers onto a hot barbecue and cook for 6–7 minutes, rotating once. Turn over and cook for a further 5–6 minutes, rotating once. At this stage, they should be cooked to medium-rare. If you want them cooked more than that just leave them on for another 1–2 minutes.

Makes 10 burgers.

SPICED BEEF BURGERS

It's easy to put your own personal stamp on burgers by adding unique ingredients to the mix, as I've done here, or by serving your very own chutney with them.

1 kg (2 lb) minced beef
½ tsp ground nutmeg
½ tsp ground cinnamon
1 tsp ground coriander
1 tsp ground cumin
1 tbsp chopped mint leaves
1 tbsp chopped coriander leaves
½ tsp salt
½ tsp freshly ground black pepper

> Mix all the ingredients together. Divide into 10 and form into burger shapes.

> Place burgers onto a hot barbecue and cook for 6–7 minutes, rotating once. Turn over and cook for a further 5–6 minutes, rotating once.

Makes 10 burgers.

BEEF BURGERS WITH ROASTED VEGETABLES

Adding a mix of roasted vegetables to beef burgers provides a real richness to the finished burger flavour.

1 onion, finely diced
1 red capsicum, finely diced
1 zucchini, finely diced
1 eggplant, finely diced
100 ml (3½ fl oz) olive oil
Salt and freshly ground black pepper
1 kg (2 lb) beef mince

> Mix the diced vegetables with the olive oil and place onto a hot barbecue plate. Cook for about 10 minutes or until the vegetables begin to soften, stirring well. When cool, mix the vegetables with the beef mince and season with salt and pepper. Divide into 10 and form into burger shapes.

> Place burgers on a hot barbecue grill and cook for 6–7 minutes, rotating once. Turn over and cook for a further 5–6 minutes, rotating once. Check burger is cooked to your preference. For more than medium-rare, cook for another 2 minutes.

Makes 10 burgers.

THAI CHICKEN BURGERS

It's simple to jazz up mince and make it more exotic. Sometimes, I just add a generous dollop of sweet chilli sauce and some breadcrumbs to chicken mince and then cook on the grill. This version is a bit more involved, but they're so popular with young and old alike that they're well worth making.

1 kg (2 lb) chicken mince
½ red capsicum, diced
¼ cup finely sliced spring onion
1 egg
1 tbsp soy sauce
1 tbsp sweet chilli sauce
2 tbsp chopped coriander
90 g (3 oz) dry breadcrumbs

> Combine the ingredients and add enough breadcrumbs to bind mixture together. Divide into 10 and form into burger shapes.

> Place burgers onto a hot barbecue and cook for 6–7 minutes, rotating once. Turn over and cook for a further 5–6 minutes, rotating once.

> Serve with extra sweet chilli sauce.

Makes 10 burgers.

CHICKEN AND VEAL BURGERS

*An Italian-inspired burger flavoured with garlic, lemon,
chopped fresh herbs and parmesan cheese.*

100 g (3½ oz) day-old bread
250 ml (8 fl oz) milk
500 g (1 lb) veal mince
500 g (1 lb) chicken mince
Salt and freshly ground black pepper
3 tbsp chopped parsley
2 garlic cloves, crushed
Zest of 1 lemon
60 g (2 oz) parmesan cheese, grated
Flour for dusting
2 lemons, cut into wedges

> Tear bread into small pieces. Soak in milk for
10–15 minutes. Squeeze well to remove excess liquid.
Place bread in a bowl, add remaining ingredients and
mix well. Divide into 10 and form into burger shapes.

> Roll each burger lightly in flour.

> Place burgers onto a hot barbecue and cook for
6–7 minutes, rotating once. Turn over and cook for a
further 5–6 minutes, rotating once.

> Serve with lemon wedges.

Makes 10 burgers.

LAMB KOFTA BURGERS

This is a great way to spice up lamb mince and make it very appealing. Serve a couple of these in some Turkish pide bread with a few spoonfuls of tomato and fresh herb salsa and you'll have a barbecue to remember.

1 kg (2 lb) lamb mince
1 onion, finely chopped
3 tsp ground coriander
4 tsp ground cumin
½ tsp ground cinnamon
½ tsp ground allspice

½ tsp ground white pepper
2 tsp oregano leaves, chopped
2 tsp harissa or chilli paste
1 tsp salt
90 g (3 oz) burghal

> Place lamb, onion, ground spices, oregano, harissa and salt in a large bowl. Knead well by hand for five minutes. Refrigerate for one hour so flavours can develop. Soak burghal in cold water for 20 minutes. Drain well. Divide mixture into 10 equal pieces and shape into burgers. Scatter burghal onto a plate and roll burgers in it until coated.

> Place burgers onto a hot barbecue and cook for 6–7 minutes, rotating once. Turn over and cook for a further 5–6 minutes, rotating once.

> At this stage they should be cooked to medium–rare. If you want them cooked more than that, just leave them on for another 2 minutes.

Makes 10 burgers.

VEAL AND ROASTED CAPSICUM BURGERS

Veal can be quite rich so I tend to add other flavours to it. Roasted capsicum provides a lovely sweetness, and the toasted pine nuts add a special crunch.

1 kg (2 lb) veal mince
1 roasted red capsicum, peeled, de-seeded and diced
60 g (2 oz) pine nuts, toasted
2 tbsp chopped basil leaves
1 tbsp tomato paste
Salt and freshly ground black pepper

> Mix all the ingredients together. Divide into 10 and form into burger shapes.

> Place burgers onto a hot barbecue and cook for 6–7 minutes, rotating once. Turn over and cook for a further 5–6 minutes, rotating once.

Makes 10 burgers.

COOKING ON THE BONE

Cooking meat and fish on the bone is a great skill to add to your repertoire. Bones help keep moisture in the food, leaving the finished product really juicy to eat. The only downside is that meats with a lot of bones also have a high fat content, and fat melts during cooking.

You'll have to keep your mind on the job, as the melting fat is just the thing to cause flare-ups and ruin your cooking. This is certainly not the outcome you're after when you're supposed to be showing off to the other assembled males. It's well worth practicing with these recipes before inviting other blokes around, until you've perfected the skills needed. The best way is to train yourself by cooking one or two chops or cutlets at a time until you've got it just right. Then, and only then, should you start showing off in front of everyone else.

There are recipes here for pork ribs, which come with thick layers of meat and thin layers of fat – perfect for barbecuing. Pork is the barbecued meat of choice in the USA, and I have included a Texan pork ribs recipe so you can experience the flavours that are popular in the southern States. There are also lots of ideas for chicken drumsticks, chops and wings, as well as fish on the bone.

But first: a word of warning regarding the infamous lamb chop. This is one of my barbecue faves, but so often I see people buy the wrong cut. Forget the bargain BBQ lamb chops promoted at markets and butcher shops. Lamb is naturally fatty, and therefore necessitates caution. It's much

You'll have to keep your mind on the job, as the melting fat is just the things to cause flare-ups and ruin your cooking.

better to go for trim lamb cuts, such as loin chops and cutlets. These cuts also love marinades and spice mixes, so there are plenty of opportunities to experiment with your own blends and mixes until you've perfected your own secret recipe.

BARBECUE PORK RIBS

This simple marinade is one of my favourites. It produces ribs that are crispy, crunchy and sticky all at the same time. How can you resist food that sounds this good?

1 kg (2 lb) pork ribs
3 tbsp tomato sauce
2 tbsp sweet chilli sauce
2 tbsp soy sauce

Place pork in a bowl. Mix tomato sauce, sweet chilli and soy sauce together. Pour over pork and marinate for 3–4 hours (time permitting).

> Drain excess marinade off before cooking.

> Place pork onto a hot barbecue and cook for 10–15 minutes, rotating and turning regularly. As the ribs cook, brush them regularly with any remaining marinade.

Serves 4.

TEXAN PORK RIBS

The Texans know a thing or two about cooking pork to perfection. If you like your ribs with a bit more zing, add a little chopped chilli to the sauce.

1 kg (2 lb) pork ribs
4 tbsp tomato sauce
1 tbsp Worcestershire sauce
1 tbsp white vinegar
1 tbsp brown sugar
2 tsp mustard
1 tsp chilli powder
½ tsp salt
¼ tsp Tabasco

> Set pork aside in a dish for marinating. Combine remaining ingredients in a saucepan and bring to the boil. Reduce to a simmer and cook for 5 minutes. Allow to cool. Pour sauce over pork and marinate for 2 hours.

> Drain excess marinade from the pork.

> Place pork onto a hot barbecue and cook for 10–15 minutes, rotating and turning regularly. During cooking, brush ribs regularly with marinade.

Serves 4.

CHINESE PORK RIBS

Asian flavours work wonderfully with pork, as you'll find when you try this easy recipe. You might like to add ginger, garlic, sesame oil or even chilli to this recipe. Experiment a little to find your favourite combination.

1 kg (2 lb) pork ribs
250 ml (8 fl oz) soy sauce
2 tbsp warm honey
½ tsp five-spice

> Place pork in a bowl. Mix soy, honey and five-spice together then marinate the pork for 2 hours.

> Drain excess marinade from the pork.

> Place pork onto a hot barbecue and cook for 10–15 minutes, rotating and turning regularly. During cooking, brush ribs regularly with marinade.

Serves 4.

TRADITIONAL LAMB CHOPS

Lamb chops come up really well with a bit of marinating, especially when this includes rosemary, lemon juice and olive oil.

3 tbsp olive oil
1 tbsp lemon juice
2 tbsp chopped fresh rosemary
Salt and freshly ground black pepper
8 lamb loin chops

> Mix oil, lemon juice, rosemary, salt and pepper together. Pour over lamb and marinate for 2 hours.

> Place lamb onto a hot barbecue and cook for 4–5 minutes, rotating once or twice. Turn over and cook for a further 3–4 minutes. Use remaining marinade for basting during cooking.

> Depending on the thickness of your chops, you may require 2–3 minutes extra cooking time, particularly if you prefer them medium rather than medium–rare.

Serves 4.

SPICED LAMB CHOPS

Lamb and spice is a perfect match, as you'll find with this recipe. You might even like to try lamb with the Indian tandoori marinade (page 70).

1 tsp sweet paprika
1 tsp ground cumin
1 tsp ground coriander
½ tsp salt
1 tbsp lemon juice
2 tbsp olive oil
8 lamb loin chops

> Mix together spices, salt, lemon juice and olive oil. Coat lamb with spice mixture.

> Place lamb onto a hot barbecue and cook for 4–5 minutes, rotating once or twice. Turn over and cook for a further 3–4 minutes. Use remaining marinade for basting during cooking.

> Depending on the thickness of your chops, you may require 2–3 minutes extra cooking time, particularly if you prefer them medium rather than medium–rare.

Serves 4.

LIP-SMACKING LIME AND CHILLI LAMB CUTLETS

Lamb cutlets, trimmed of excess fat and marinated in lime and chilli are always a hit for a weekday family dinner. Everyone – and I mean everyone – loves them.

3 tbsp lime juice
1 small red chilli, de-seeded and finely diced
1 tsp caster sugar
½ tsp salt
2 tbsp olive oil
12 trim lamb cutlets

> Whisk the lime juice, chilli, sugar, salt and olive oil together. Brush liberally onto lamb cutlets and marinate for 30 minutes (time permitting).

> Place lamb onto a hot barbecue and cook for 4–5 minutes, rotating once or twice. Turn over and cook for a further 3–4 minutes. Use remaining marinade for basting during cooking.

Makes 12.

TEXAN CHICKEN DRUMSTICKS

*The flavours in this Texan mix are perfect on chicken
drumsticks. Cooking on the bone also leaves the chicken
beautifully moist to eat.*

1 garlic clove, crushed
1 tsp chilli powder
1 tsp sweet paprika
1 tsp mustard
½ tsp ground coriander
½ tsp ground cumin
½ tsp freshly ground black pepper
½ tsp salt
2 tbsp olive oil
1 kg (2 lb) chicken drumsticks

> Mix the garlic, chilli, paprika, mustard, coriander,
cumin, pepper, salt and olive oil together. Rub this
over the chicken drumsticks and marinate for
30 minutes (time permitting).

> Place drumsticks onto a hot barbecue and cook for
30 minutes, turning often. Use remaining marinade
for basting during cooking.

Serves 5–6.

THAI COCONUT CHICKEN CHOPS

Chicken chops are from the thigh and have only one bone remaining, making them both juicy and easy to eat.

2 tbsp red Thai curry paste
200 ml (7 fl oz) coconut cream
1 kg (2 lb) chicken chops

> Place curry paste and coconut cream in a small saucepan. Bring to the boil and simmer for a couple of minutes. Add salt to taste. Brush the cooled marinade on the chicken chops.

> Place chicken chops onto a hot barbecue and cook for 20 minutes, turning often. Use remaining marinade for basting during cooking.

Serves 4.

CHERMOULA CHICKEN WINGS

A brilliant combination of tasty chicken with a wonderful spice mixture. Try it just once and you'll be an instant fan, guaranteed.

1 kg (2 lb) chicken wings

2 tsp sweet paprika

1 tsp ground ginger

1 tsp chilli powder

1 tsp ground cumin

1 tsp ground coriander

1 tsp ground white pepper

½ tsp ground cardamom

½ tsp ground cinnamon

½ tsp allspice

1 tsp salt

2 tbsp lemon juice

3 tbsp olive oil

> Place the chicken wings into a large dish. Mix all of the remaining ingredients together to form a smooth paste. Rub this over the chicken wings and marinate for 30 minutes (time permitting).

> Place chicken wings onto a hot barbecue and cook for 20 minutes, turning often.

Serves 5–6.

CORIANDER, CHILLI AND LIME SARDINES

Sardines are the perfect thing to serve up at a barbecue when guests are first arriving. They cook in just a couple of minutes and taste brilliant.

1 peeled garlic clove
2 tsp toasted coriander seeds
1 small red chilli, finely diced
1 tbsp lime juice
2 tbsp olive oil
Salt and freshly ground black pepper
20 sardines, gutted

> Place the garlic, coriander seeds and chilli in a food processor and mix until smooth. Add the lime juice, olive oil, salt and pepper.

> Brush the marinade over the sardines and marinate for 1 hour (time permitting).

> Cook sardines on a hot barbecue plate for 2–3 minutes on each side.

Makes 20.

MINTY SALMON CUTLETS

Sounds odd but believe me: it's delicious. Try it once and you may even find yourself addicted.

½ cup mint leaves
4 spring onions, roughly chopped
2 small green chillies, finely diced
1 tsp grated ginger
1 tsp caster sugar
1 tbsp lime juice
2 tbsp oil
6 salmon cutlets

> Place the mint leaves, onion, chilli, ginger, and sugar into a food processor and mix until smooth. Add the lime juice and olive oil.

> Brush the marinade over the salmon and marinate for 1 hour (time permitting).

> Place salmon onto a hot barbecue plate and cook for 3–4 minutes. Turn the salmon over and cook for a further 3 minutes.

Serves 6.

COOKING KEBABS

Kebabs are a winner with barbecue cooks and guests alike. For the cook, they offer a strong link with early barbecuing: I mean what could be more primitive than using a piece of wood to hold a chunk of meat over the coals to cook?

Cooking kebabs requires a high degree of barbecuing skill as they cook very quickly. You'll need to learn when is just the right time to turn them and, if you're using wooden skewers, to watch that they don't get burnt by the coals.

All of this can only be learned through experience; by cooking different types of kebabs until you get it just right. Virtually any type of meat or seafood can be used on a kebab, and these tiny morsels are an easy way to try out new tastes and flavours. So take the time to explore all the options available to you.

You could start out by practising with something as simple as a plain chicken or beef kebab, maybe brushed with a little olive oil and lemon juice, salt and pepper. Then you could move onwards and upwards to chicken tandoori kebabs, or some tender lamb fillet scented with fresh rosemary. The next challenge could be Moroccan spiced lamb kebabs or go Chinese with some black bean and sesame marinated pork kebabs.

Guests at a barbecue love kebabs too as they dispense with the need for a knife and fork: you just hang onto the skewer and enjoy.

The choice of bamboo or metal skewers is yours alone to make. Wooden skewers need to be soaked in cold water for at least 1 hour before use to ensure they won't burn, whereas metal skewers require no preparation. Flat metal skewers have the added advantage that the meat won't spin while you're trying to turn them; the bonus with bamboo is that you won't have to wash up afterwards.

Virtually any type of meat or seafood can be used on a kebab, and these tiny morsels are an easy way to try out new tastes and flavours. So take the time to explore all the options available to you.

▬ ▬ ▬ ▬ ▬ ▬ ▬ ▬ ▬ ▬ ▬ ▬ ▬ ▬ ▬

SIMPLE CHICKEN KEBABS

This is your classic chicken kebab recipe and it's what beginners should practice with until they get the hang of kebabs. Once they've been mastered, try the marinades on page 69–72.

500 g (1 lb) chicken fillets, skin removed
2 tbsp olive oil
Salt and freshly ground black pepper
8 skewers

> Cut chicken into 2 cm (¾ in) chunks. Mix the chicken with the olive oil and salt and pepper. Thread 6–7 pieces of chicken onto each skewer.

> Place kebabs onto a hot barbecue and cook for 10 minutes, turning 2–3 times.

Makes 8 kebabs.

CHICKEN AND PROSCIUTTO KEBABS

This is an Italian-inspired combination of chicken marinated in olive oil and sage, then wrapped in prosciutto ham. They've always proved a big hit at my barbies.

500 g (1 lb) chicken fillets, skin removed
2 tbsp olive oil
2 tbsp chopped fresh sage
Salt and freshly ground black pepper
30 thin slices prosciutto
8 skewers

> Cut each chicken fillet into 2 cm (¾ in) chunks. Mix the chicken with the oil, sage, salt and pepper and marinate for 1 hour.

> Cut prosciutto slices in half lengthways. Wrap each chunk of chicken up in a slice of prosciutto. Thread 6–7 pieces of wrapped chicken onto each skewer.

> Place kebabs onto a hot barbecue and cook for 10 minutes, turning 2–3 times.

Makes 8 kebabs.

CHICKEN TANDOORI KEBABS

Tandoori is an incredibly popular Indian dish, and one that suits barbecuing really well. You can serve these kebabs as they are, or go all out and get some naan bread from your local Indian take away. Then, just serve the meat in the bread with a dollop of yoghurt and perhaps a little sliced lettuce, tomato and cucumber.

500 g (1 lb) chicken fillets, skin removed
2 tbsp natural yoghurt
2 tbsp tandoori paste
1 tbsp lemon juice
8 skewers
Naan bread, extra yoghurt, lettuce, tomato and
  cucumber as required

> Dice chicken into 2 cm (¾ in) chunks. Mix the chicken with yoghurt, tandoori paste and lemon juice and marinate for 1 hour.

> Thread 6–7 pieces of chicken onto each skewer.

> Place kebabs onto a hot barbecue and cook for 10 minutes, turning 2–3 times. Serve as they are or in nann bread with all the trimmings.

Makes 8 kebabs.

ROSEMARY LAMB KEBABS

Lamb always cooks well on the barbecue. It can cope with high temperatures without drying out – as long as it isn't overcooked, of course. Rosemary is a flavour that has long been associated with lamb and it's terrific here too. For extra rosemary flavour, thread the lamb onto rosemary branches instead of skewers.

500 g (1 lb) leg of lamb leg or lamb fillets
1–2 tbsp olive oil
1 tbsp lemon juice
2 tbsp chopped fresh rosemary
Salt and freshly ground black pepper
8 skewers

> Dice lamb into 2 cm (¾ in) chunks. Mix the lamb with the remaining ingredients then marinate for up to 2 hours (time permitting).

> Thread 6–7 pieces of lamb onto each skewer or rosemary branch.

> Place kebabs onto a hot barbecue and cook for 8 minutes, turning 3–4 times.

Makes 8 kebabs.

NORTH AFRICAN SPICED LAMB KEBABS

This combination of fragrant spices and lamb is based on a classic North African kebab recipe. Try them once and you'll realise they're an absolute winner.

500 g (1 lb) leg of lamb leg or lamb fillets
1 tsp ground coriander
1 tsp ground cumin
1 tsp sweet paprika
½ tsp salt
1½ tbsp lemon juice
2 tbsp olive oil
8 skewers

> Dice lamb into 2 cm (¾ in) chunks. Mix the lamb with the remaining ingredients then marinate for up to 2 hours (time permitting).

> Thread 6–7 pieces of lamb onto each skewer.

> Place kebabs onto a hot barbecue and cook for 8 minutes, turning 3–4 times.

Makes 8 kebabs.

CLASSIC BEEF, MUSHROOM AND CAPSICUM KEBABS

When making beef kebabs it pays to use a tender cut of beef. I always use rump steak, porterhouse or even fillet – if the budget allows.

500 g (1 lb) tender beef, such as fillet,
    porterhouse or rump
2 tsp mustard
2 tsp chopped fresh rosemary
2 tbsp olive oil
2 tbsp red wine
Salt and freshly ground black pepper
1 red capsicum, halved, de-seeded and cut into
    2 cm ($^3/_4$ in) dice
200g (7 oz) button mushrooms, wiped clean
    and cut in half
10 skewers

> Cut the beef into 2 cm (¾ in) chunks. Mix the mustard, rosemary, olive oil, red wine, salt and pepper together and marinate the beef for 1 hour.

> Drain excess marinade from the beef then thread the beef, capsicum and mushrooms onto the skewers.

> Place kebabs on a hot barbecue grill and cook for 12 minutes, turning 3–4 times.

Makes 10 kebabs.

CHINESE PORK KEBABS WITH BLACK BEAN AND SESAME

Pork has its own built-in fat that keeps it beautifully moist when barbecued. Try these kebabs to discover how good it can be.

500 g (1 lb) pork fillet
1 tbsp black beans, soaked in cold water
    for 10 minutes, then drained
2 tsp sesame oil
2 tbsp soy sauce
2 tsp grated ginger
8 skewers

> Dice pork into 2 cm (¾ in) chunks. Mash black beans with a fork, then add remaining ingredients. Mix the pork with the marinade for up to 2 hours (time permitting).

> Thread 6–7 pieces of pork onto each skewer.

> Place kebabs onto a hot barbecue and cook for 8 minutes, turning 3–4 times.

Makes 8 kebabs.

PEPPERED KANGAROO KEBABS

Kangaroo is Australia's own wild meat and it tastes incredible when cooked on the barbecue. Low in saturated fat, kangaroo is ideal if your doctor is giving you a hard time about reducing your cholesterol.

500 g (1 lb) kangaroo meat
1 tbsp red wine
1 tbsp olive oil
1 tsp salt
1 tbsp freshly ground black pepper
8 skewers

> Dice kangaroo into 2 cm (¾ in) chunks. Mix meat, red wine and oil together. Marinate for 30 minutes.

> Thread 6–7 pieces of kangaroo onto each skewer and sprinkle with salt and pepper. Place kebabs onto a hot barbecue and cook for 8 minutes, turning 3–4 times. Rest for 5 minutes before serving.

Makes 8 kebabs.

SOY AND GINGER SALMON KEBABS

Many barbecue cooks avoid fish at all costs – probably because they think it will fall apart when they try to cook it. Fish such as salmon, is ideal for barbecuing as it holds its shape perfectly during cooking. This marinade makes a wonderful Asian-flavoured crust on the fish and adds a gutsy flavour.

500 g (1 lb) salmon fillet, skin removed
1 tsp grated ginger
1 small red chilli, de-seeded and finely diced
1 tbsp kecap manis
3 tbsp soy sauce
3 tbsp peanut oil
8 skewers

> Dice salmon into 2 cm (¾ in) chunks. Mix remaining ingredients together. Pour over salmon and marinate for 1 hour.

> Drain salmon well and reserve remaining marinade for basting. Thread 6–7 pieces of salmon onto each skewer.

> Place kebabs onto a hot barbecue and cook for 8–10 minutes, turning 3–4 times.

> Baste with reserve marinade while cooking.

Makes 8 kebabs.

TUNA TERIYAKI KEBABS

Tuna is another firm fish that suits barbecuing really well. Tuna has natural oils so it stays juicy too. Try not to cook the tuna for more than 4–5 minutes or it will dry out. Try these kebabs just once and they're sure to become a favourite.

500 g (1 lb) tuna, skin removed
4 tbsp soy sauce
2 tbsp mirin
2 tsp grated ginger
1 tsp sesame oil
1 tsp caster sugar
8 skewers

> Cut tuna into 2 cm (¾ in) chunks. Mix the remaining ingredients together. Pour marinade over the tuna and marinate for 30 minutes.

> Drain tuna well then thread 6–7 chunks of tuna onto each skewer.

> Place tuna kebabs onto a hot barbecue plate and cook for 4–5 minutes, turning over once.

Makes 8 kebabs.

CAJUN BARBECUED PRAWN KEBABS

Paul Hogan told the world that we love throwing a shrimp on the barbie, so who are we to argue? Prawns cook well as kebabs because the skewers hold them flat on the grill, which also makes them really easy to eat.

1 kg (2 lb) green (raw) prawns
30 skewers
1 tbsp sweet paprika
1 tbsp onion powder
1 tbsp garlic powder
2 tsp ground thyme
2 tsp ground oregano
1 tsp cayenne pepper
1 tsp white pepper
1 tsp freshly ground black pepper
2 limes, cut into wedges

> Shell and de-vein prawns. Thread one prawn onto each skewer lengthways. Mix the remaining ingredients together and sprinkle generously onto the kebabs.

> Place prawns onto a hot barbecue and cook for 3–4 minutes on each side.

> Serve with lime wedges.

Makes 30 kebabs.

Prawn kebabs also taste fantastic rubbed with Chermoula spice mix (page 68) and the gutsy black bean and chilli marinade (page 69).

BACON AND SCALLOP KEBABS

Scallops are usually too delicate to cope with the heat of a barbecue. However, wrap them in bacon and they'll end up tender, juicy and delicious.

500 g (1 lb) scallops
30 thin slices streaky (back) bacon
Freshly ground black pepper
8 skewers

> Sort through your scallops and ensure there aren't any vagrant shell pieces. Cut slices of bacon in two and wrap a piece around each scallop.

> Place 6–7 bacon-wrapped scallops onto each skewer. Grind lots of black pepper over kebabs.

> Place scallop kebabs onto a hot barbecue and cook for 4–5 minutes, turning 2–3 times.

Makes 8 kebabs.

COOKING THE PERFECT STEAK

A perfectly cooked steak – one with a golden crust on the surface and packed with pink, meaty juices – is one of the greatest food pleasures your barbecue can offer. Cooking the perfect steak is one of the essential skills a barbecue cook needs to learn. There are many tricks of the trade when cooking a steak, many of which you'll learn here.

When hunting your steak, there are a few things to look for to ensure it is going to be perfect:

- The meat should be bright red

- There should be a nice layer of creamy fat across the top of the steak

- The meat should have some marbling running through it, as this will ensure the cooked steak is juicy to eat.

A good steak doesn't need much adornment. As Flacco the clown once said: 'Get that bloody parsley off!' If you must add something, keep it simple. A quick brush of olive oil and a light seasoning with salt

A good steak doesn't need much adornment. As Flacco the clown once said: 'Get that bloody parsley off!'

━━ ━━ ━━ ━━ ━━ ━━ ━━ ━━ ━━ ━━ ━━ ━━ ━━ ━━

and freshly ground black pepper is often enough. Perhaps rub a little seeded mustard over the steak before cooking, or a little chilli paste or freshly ground black pepper. You could also try serving your steak with a homemade mustard or chutney.

A really hot barbecue is an essential key to producing steak that makes your mouth water. This ensures a good, golden crust will form on the meat; the temperature can be lowered after the initial cooking part.

No matter how tempting it is to put the tongs to good use, it's essential you let the steak cook on one side before turning it over. If you constantly flip-flop the steak around there's no way it can cook correctly.

The typical steak is around 2 cm (¾ in) thick. This will need about 6 minutes on the first side and a further 4–5 minutes on the other side. Juices will start to appear on top of the steak: this is your best guide to turn a steak over. This will produce a steak cooked to medium–rare.

It is also important to let steak rest in a cool part of the barbecue for 5 minutes before serving. This will allow the juices to be retained in the meat when it is cut and produce a juicier steak.

Don't forget other foods also come as steaks too. That is, basically, a thick slice of meat or fish, free of bone.

Juices will start to appear on top of the steak: this is your best guide to turn a steak over.

━ ━ ━ ━ ━ ━ ━

IS IT COOKED?

A fantastic skill to learn is how to tell if a steak is cooked by pressing it with your finger or a pair or tongs. Once mastered, this is a great party trick to show off to your mates. It's well worth practising until you've perfected it.

- Press into raw meat and it will feel like soft butter.

- Press into meat that is cooked to rare and it will feel like a sponge.

- Press into meat that is cooked to medium–rare and it will feel like the fleshy base of your thumb.

- Press into meat that is cooked to medium and it will feel like the base of your middle finger.

- Press into meat that is cooked to well done and it will be as solid as a rock. Avoid this at all costs.

COOKING THE PERFECT PORTERHOUSE STEAK

Porterhouse steak is one of the most commonly seen barbecue steaks. It offers a great balance between flavour and juiciness, with a nice layer of fat across the top to keep it moist during cooking.

1 porterhouse steak per person, approximately 200 g (7 oz) each and 2 cm (¾ in) thick

> Brush steak with olive oil to ensure it will not stick to the grill. Season with salt and pepper if desired. Place porterhouse steak onto a hot barbecue and cook for 6 minutes, rotating as needed.

> Turn steak over and cook for a further 4–5 minutes, rotating as needed.

> Allow the steak to rest in a cool part of the barbecue for 5 minutes before serving.

COOKING THE PERFECT RUMP STEAK

Rump is a gutsy, full-flavoured meat that is perfectly suited to barbecuing.

Rump steaks often weigh up to 500g (1 lb) each and may need to be cut in half for a regular portion. Alternatively, prove your manhood and eat the whole thing!

1 rump steak per person, approximately 250g (8 oz) each and 2 cm (¾ in) thick

> Brush steak with olive oil to ensure it will not stick to the grill and season with salt and pepper if desired.

> Place rump steak onto a hot barbecue and cook for 6 minutes, rotating as needed.

> Turn steak over and cook for a further 4–5 minutes, rotating as needed.

> Allow the steak to rest on a cool part of the barbecue for 5 minutes before serving.

COOKING THE PERFECT SCOTCH FILLET STEAK

Scotch fillet steak is one of the most economical cuts of beef available. It offers a fairly mild beefy flavour with a decent amount of fat in the meat to keep it moist during cooking.

1 scotch fillet steak per person, approximately 200 g (7 oz)
    each and 2 cm (¾ in) thick

> Brush steak with olive oil to ensure it will not stick to the grill and season with salt and pepper if desired.

> Place scotch fillet steak onto a hot barbecue and cook for 6 minutes, rotating as needed.

> Turn steak over and cook for a further 4–5 minutes, rotating as needed.

> Allow the steak to rest in a cool part of the barbecue for 5 minutes before serving.

COOKING THE PERFECT T-BONE STEAK

T-bone steak is a real meat-lover's steak. It demands a big appetite as they usually weigh in at about 400–500g (¾–1 lb) each.

They have a distinctive T-shaped bone down the centre, with porterhouse on one side and eye fillet on the other.

1 T-bone steak per person, approximately 400g–500g
   (¾–1 lb) each

> Brush steak with olive oil to ensure it will not stick to the grill and season with salt and pepper if desired.

> Place T-bone steak onto a hot barbecue and cook for 6 minutes, rotating as needed.

> Turn steak over and cook for a further 5–6 minutes, rotating as needed.

> Allow the steak to rest in a cool part of the barbecue for 5 minutes before serving.

COOKING THE PERFECT FILLET STEAK

Fillet steak is often known as eye fillet. It is the prime beef cut with very little visible fat, no waste and it is incredibly tender. It is neither too mild nor too strong. Fillet steak is often quite thick and will need a longer cooking time than most other steaks.

1 fillet steak per person, approximately 200 g (2¾ in) each, and up to 7 cm (2¾ in) thick

> Brush steak with olive oil to ensure it will not stick to the grill and season with salt and pepper if desired.

> Place fillet steak onto a hot barbecue and cook for 10 minutes, rotating as needed.

> Turn steak over and cook for a further 8 minutes, rotating as needed.

> Allow the steak to rest in a cool part of the barbecue for 5 minutes before serving.

COOKING THE PERFECT RIB OF BEEF

Rib of beef is simply fillet steak still attached to a rib bone. It is one of the most delicious steaks to cook on the barbecue because cooking meat on the bone produces a juicier end product.

1 rib of beef per person, approx 400g (13 oz) each

> Brush steak with olive oil to ensure it will not stick to the grill and season with salt and pepper if desired.

> Place the rib of beef onto a hot barbecue and cook for 10 minutes, rotating as needed.

> Turn steak over and cook for a further 8–9 minutes, rotating as needed.

> Allow the steak to rest in a cool part of the barbecue for 5 minutes before serving.

JAPANESE GLAZED STEAK

This glaze will create a beautiful crust on barbecued steak.

2 tbsp soy sauce
1 tbsp mirin
1 tsp grated ginger

> Mix the soy, mirin and ginger together and brush it onto steaks as they cook.

CHIMICHURI

This traditional marinade recipe from Argentina is brilliant on beef. Try it spooned over a steak, beef ribs or virtually any barbecued beef. It also makes a brilliant basting sauce for a spit roast. Thanks for the recipe Stella.

3 tbsp finely chopped onion
2 tbsp finely chopped
   thyme or oregano
½ tsp sweet paprika
Salt and freshly ground
   black pepper

1 garlic clove, crushed
2 tbsp olive oil
2 tbsp white wine vinegar
¼ cup finely chopped parsley

> Mix everything together and season with salt and pepper.

MAPLE SYRUP AND MUSTARD GLAZE

This glaze will add a great sweet mustard crust to any barbecued steak.

2 tbsp maple syrup
1 tbsp mustard
Salt and freshly ground black pepper

> Mix the maple syrup and mustard together and add a little salt and pepper. Brush it onto steaks as they cook.

GARLIC BUTTER #1

Garlic butter is a classic accompaniment to good steak. In this recipe, the melted garlic butter is kept in a bowl on the side of the barbecue and brushed onto the meat as it cooks. It's pure unadulterated pleasure.

100 g (3½ oz) soft butter
2 garlic cloves, crushed
3 tbsp chopped herbs
Salt and freshly ground black pepper

> Mix together butter, garlic, herbs, salt and pepper in a small heatproof bowl. When you're ready to cook, place this bowl onto a cool part of the barbecue so it can melt. Simply brush the steaks a few times on each side as they cook.

GARLIC BUTTER #2

This is the more traditional way of serving garlic butter. Here, it's rolled up in greaseproof paper, chilled, then sliced to serve on top of a sizzling steak.

100g (3½ oz) soft butter
2 garlic cloves, crushed
3 tbsp chopped herbs
Salt and freshly ground black pepper

> Mix butter, garlic, herbs, salt and black pepper together.

> Place onto a sheet of greaseproof paper and roll into a tube shape. Chill until needed. Slice the butter and place onto each steak as they come from the barbecue.

ANCHOVY BUTTER

This may sound like an unusual combination but the anchovies are so deliciously salty that they taste brilliant on barbecued steak. Go on, what have you got to lose?

100 g (3½ oz) soft butter
25 g (¾ oz) anchovies, chopped
1 tbsp lemon juice
Finely chopped zest of 1 lemon
1 tbsp chopped parsley leaves
½ tsp freshly ground black pepper

> Mix butter, anchovies, lemon juice and zest, parsley and black pepper together.

> Place onto a sheet of greaseproof paper and roll into a tube shape. Chill until needed.

> Slice the butter and place onto each steak as they come from the barbecue.

SIMPLE HERB CHICKEN FILLETS

This is oh so easy to do: just a few chicken fillets on the grill to watch over and a simple herb seasoning to brush over them from time to time.

2 tbsp olive oil
3 tbsp chopped herbs
Salt and freshly ground black pepper
4 chicken fillets

> Mix the olive oil, herbs, salt and pepper together. Brush the fillets with a little of the herb seasoning.

> Place onto a hot barbecue and cook for 6 minutes, rotating once.

> Baste the fillets with the herb seasoning from time to time.

> Turn over and cook for a further 4–6 minutes, rotating once.

Serves 4.

BARBECUE CHICKEN SALAD

One great thing about using steak cuts is they can be barbecued, then sliced and placed over the top of a salad. This makes what is known as a warm salad. It's a great way of serving meat with plenty of fresh salad ingredients.

2 chicken breast fillets
Olive oil for cooking
400 g (13 oz) salad mix, washed
100 g (3½ oz) feta cheese, diced
100 g (3½ oz) kalamata olives
1 avocado, sliced
½ punnet cherry tomatoes, halved
12 basil leaves
1 tbsp vinegar
3 tbsp olive oil

> Brush the fillets with a little olive oil, place onto a hot barbecue and cook for 6 minutes, rotating once. Turn over and cook for a further 4–6 minutes, rotating once. Allow chicken to rest on a cool part of the barbecue for 5 mins.

> Place the salad mix onto a large platter then scatter the feta cheese, olives, avocado, cherry tomatoes and basil over the top. Slice the cooked chicken and spread it on top of the salad. Mix the vinegar and olive oil together and drizzle over the top. Serve immediately.

Serves 4–6.

BARBECUE BEEF SALAD WITH LIME DRESSING

This is another great example of using barbecued steak to make a fresh and delicious salad. It's a great way of serving quite a few people with just a couple of steaks.

2 x 200g (7 oz) porterhouse steaks
250 g (8 oz) rocket leaves
½ punnet cherry tomatoes, halved
1 avocado, sliced
2 tbsp lime juice
4 tbsp peanut oil
1 tsp soy sauce
½ tsp fish sauce

> Place porterhouse steak onto a hot barbecue and cook for 6 minutes, rotating as needed. Turn steak over and cook for a further 4–5 minutes, rotating as needed. Allow the steak to rest in a cool part of the barbecue for 5 minutes.

> Arrange rocket on a platter, and top with the cherry tomatoes and avocado slices. Whisk together the lime juice, peanut oil, soy sauce and fish sauce. Slice the steaks and spread over the salad before topping with dressing. Serve immediately.

Serves 4–6.

CHERMOULA SPICE SALMON STEAKS

Chermoula is one of my favourite spice mixes: it's so flavoursome and complex. I adore it on chicken wings, prawns and salmon.

4 x 200 g (7 oz) salmon steaks
2 tsp sweet paprika
1 tsp ground ginger
1 tsp chilli powder
1 tsp ground cumin
1 tsp ground coriander
1 tsp ground white pepper
½ tsp ground cardamom
½ tsp ground cinnamon
½ tsp allspice
1 tsp salt
2 tbsp lemon juice
3 tbsp olive oil

> Place the salmon steaks into a bowl for marinating. Mix the remaining ingredients together to form a smooth paste. Brush spice paste over both sides of the salmon fillets. Leave to marinate for 30 minutes (time permitting).

> Place salmon onto a hot barbecue grill and cook for 5 minutes, rotating once.

> Turn over and cook for a further 4 minutes, rotating once.

Serves 4.

BARBECUED FISH FILLETS

Fish fillets such as flathead, blue eye, tuna and salmon are all excellent on the barbecue. They'll be much easier to cook on a flat plate than a grill.

2 tbsp butter
2 tsp chopped fresh herbs
Zest of 1 lemon, chopped
Freshly ground black pepper
4 x 200 g (7 oz) firm white fish fillets

> Combine the butter, herbs, lemon zest and pepper together in a heatproof bowl. Place it in a warm spot on the side on the barbecue to melt.

> Brush the fish with a little melted butter then place onto the hot barbecue plate. Cook for 3–4 minute, basting fish regularly with the butter. Turn over and cook for a further 4–5 minutes.

Serves 4.

COOKING WHOLE THINGS

Virtually anyone can learn how to barbecue a few sausages, a couple of lamb chops or a few steaks. This chapter, however, takes the barbecue enthusiast into the serious end of the business. It's an area where many new skills are required; it's where the cuts of meat and types of fish to be barbecued are quite different. *How* the barbecue is used is also quite different to the usual grill skills.

Accepting the challenge to cook in this way is big step, and one that most men are not willing to take – mostly because the failure of serving up meat with a raw centre or having a whole fish fall apart as it's served is too much to cope with. This is a step to be taken seriously, so pay attention!

For those willing to strike out into new territory, the rewards are enormous. With a bit of effort you can soon be brushing whole chicken with a delicious mixture of lemon juice and fresh herbs as it cooks to a succulent golden brown. Then you can move onto a boned leg of lamb that has been rubbed with garlic and olive oil and slowly sizzled until pink and tender. Or perhaps a neck of pork brushed with just the right amount of soy, honey and chilli to allow a tasty crust to form. Mm.

But wait there's more. You can barbecue a whole salmon over glowing coals until it's transformed into moist, pink smoky fish.

Cooking whole things takes the barbecue enthusiast into the serious end of the business.

On Christmas day you can serve up a whole turkey that has been coated with Moroccan spices and slow cooked for two hours. Cooking large pieces of meat – particularly meat on the bone – produces full-flavoured, juicy meat that will make you proud to be a man.

The temperature of the barbecue where whole things are cooking needs to be low–medium in order to allow the meat time to cook through without burning the outside. Because of the size and weight of the foods to be cooked, it'll need close attention from the barbecue cook.

These foods will also need the barbecue cook to work with both tongs and a spatula to lift the food from the barbecue to the serving platters. This will take quite a bit of practice to ensure you don't totally embarrass yourself (not to mention ruining your meal) by dropping it halfway. Master the skills of cooking whole things and you'll soon be on the path to the Holy Grail of barbecuing – the spit roast!

COOKING WITH A LID

Cooking whole things using a barbecue basically involves putting a lid over the food in order to speed up the cooking time. This could be a large metal lid, such as those supplied with kettle barbecues and some trolley barbecues.

If your trolley barbecue doesn't have a lid, or you are using an open-fire barbecue, you can easily use a lid from a wok or even a large piece of foil. A deep baking tray, or large metal mixing bowls, are also good substitutes.

PREPARING POULTRY

Poultry can be cooked whole in a large barbecue, but an even easier way is to cut them through the backbone and press them flat. To do this:

- Place the bird breast-side-up on a chopping board

- Insert a sharp knife into the cavity and cut firmly through the backbone

- Turn the bird skin-side-down and trim away rib bones as desired

- The easier option is to ask your butcher to do it: ring in advance and ask him nicely

BARBECUE CHICKEN

Barbecued chicken will taste great just brushed with a little olive oil, and sprinkled with salt and freshly ground black pepper. For even more flavour, try the garlic butter or the lemon and herb baste on page 132.

1.6 kg (3 lb) chicken, cut through the backbone
  and pressed flat
1–2 tbsp olive oil
Salt and freshly ground black pepper

> Rub chicken all over with olive oil and salt and pepper. Place onto a hot barbecue. Cover with a lid and cook for 15 minutes, rotating as required.

> Turn chicken over and re-cover. Cook for a further 15 minutes, rotating as required. Remove lid, and cook uncovered for the final 10 minutes.

> Allow the chicken to rest in a cool part of the barbecue for 5 minutes before serving. Cut chicken into portions as required.

Serves 4.

[Note: if you are using a marinade or baste, simply brush this on a few times on each side as it cooks. There will be no need to use the olive oil, salt and pepper.]

GARLIC BUTTER

Garlic butter is one of those classic flavours that everybody loves and when brushed onto barbecuing food, it's pure magic. It also helps the skin of a chicken cook to a golden crackling crispness.

100 g (3½ oz) soft butter   2 garlic cloves, crushed
3 tbsp chopped herbs
Salt and freshly ground black pepper

> Mix together butter, garlic, herbs, salt and pepper in a small heatproof bowl. When you're ready to cook, place this bowl onto a warm part of the barbecue so it can melt. Simply brush the chicken a few times on each side as it cooks.

LEMON AND HERB BASTE

This is one of my all time favourites, especially on chicken. It's a great mix of garlic, herbs and lemon juice with just a hint of spice.

2 garlic cloves, crushed
½ cup chopped herbs – parsley, thyme, basil
   and oregano are great
1 tbsp lemon juice
Salt and freshly ground black pepper
Pinch of ground cumin
Pinch of ground coriander
Pinch of sweet paprika
3 tbsp olive oil

> Mix the ingredients together and brush onto your chicken a few times on each side as it cooks.

BARBECUE QUAIL

*Quails are brilliant on the barbie for a number of reasons.
Because they're small, they're quick to cook and
inexpensive to buy. Being cooked on the bone, they're
always juicy too. Because of their size they won't even
require a lid to cook them through. Try them with the
cumin and lemon baste on page 134 and serve two per
person.*

1–2 quails per person, approximately 200 g (7 oz) each,
    cut through the backbone and pressed flat
2 tbsp olive oil
Salt and freshly ground black pepper

> Rub quails all over with olive oil and salt and
pepper. Place onto a hot barbecue. Cook for 5
minutes, rotating as required.

> Turn over, baste lightly and cook for a further
5 minutes, rotating as required.

> Allow the quail to rest in a cool part of the barbecue
for 2–3 minutes before cutting in half along the
breastbone to serve.

*[Note: if you are using a marinade or baste, simply brush
this on a few times on each side as it cooks. There will be no
need to use the olive oil, salt and pepper.]*

CUMIN AND LEMON BASTE

This baste is pretty gutsy in flavour and works well with quail and duck.

2 tbsp lemon juice
3 tsp ground cumin
1 tsp toasted cumin seeds
1 tsp caster sugar
½ tsp salt
1 tsp harissa or chilli sauce
2 tbsp olive oil

> Mix the ingredients together and brush onto quail or duck as it barbecues.

BARBECUE DUCK

Duck is tricky to cook on the barbecue, mostly because of the high amount of fat released during cooking. This creates quite a challenge for the barbecue cook to ensure this fat does not create flare-ups and burn the duck. The best way around it is to cook the duck in a kettle barbecue with the coals pushed to one side or on the flat plate of a trolley barbecue. Pay close attention as the duck cooks and move it away from flames if they appear.

2 kg (4 lb) duck, cut through the backbone and pressed flat
1–2 tbsp olive oil
Salt and freshly ground black pepper

> Rub duck all over with olive oil and salt and pepper and place onto a hot barbecue. Cover and cook for 15 minutes, rotating as required.

> Turn duck over and re-cover. Cook for a further 15 minutes, rotating as required.

> Remove lid and cook uncovered for the final 10 minutes.

> Allow the duck to rest in a cool part of the barbecue for 5 minutes before serving. Cut into portions as required.

Serves 4.

[Note: if you are using a marinade or baste, simply brush this on a few times on each side as it cooks. There will be no need to use the olive oil, salt and pepper.]

JAPANESE GLAZE

This glaze produces a duck with a distinctive Japanese flavour and a stunning hint of orange.

3 tbsp soy sauce
1 tsp sesame oil
1 tbsp mirin
3 tbsp orange juice

> Mix the ingredients together and marinate for 1–2 hours. Brush remaining marinade onto duck as it cooks.

TEA-SCENTED STICKY DUCK MARINADE

This combination of flavours – Asian in origin– is brilliant on duck. The duck requires around 4 hours of marinating to fully take on the subtle flavours.

1 tbsp jasmine tea
2 star anise
250 ml (8 fl oz) boiling water
3 tbsp honey
10 cm (4 in) ginger, peeled and thinly sliced

> Combine tea and star anise and pour boiling water over. Brew for 5 minutes, then strain. Allow tea to cool. Mix the tea, honey and ginger together and pour over the duck. Marinate for 4 hours.

> Drain excess marinade from duck before placing onto the barbecue and brush this occasionally onto the duck as it cooks.

MOROCCAN BARBECUED TURKEY

This is one of my favourite ways to serve turkey on Christmas day, mostly because it tastes brilliant and is super easy to prepare. It's that mantra of minimum effort for maximum flavour. You could, of course, simply rub the bird with olive oil and salt and pepper.

This is one recipe that I believe is best cooked in a kettle barbecue due to the size of a turkey. Only here do you get the long, even cooking temperature that you require.

1 turkey or turkey buffet 3.5–4 kg (7–8 lb)
4 tsp ground cumin
2 tsp ground ginger
½ tsp ground cinnamon
Pinch of ground cloves
4 tsp ground coriander
¼ tsp freshly ground black pepper
2 pinches saffron threads, approx 20
½ tsp salt
3 tbsp olive oil

> Pat the turkey dry, then mix all of the spices together with the olive oil. Brush mixture over the skin of the turkey.

> Place turkey on a baking tray and place it in your hot kettle barbecue. Cover and cook for 2–2½ hours in total. To test the meat, insert a knife into the thickest part of the meat then remove it. If the juices that come from the cut are clear, the meat is ready. If the juices are red, the meat requires a little more cooking.

> Remove turkey from the barbecue when ready, cover with foil and rest for 20 minutes before carving.

Serves 12.

BARBECUE FILLET OF BEEF

There's something incredibly impressive about throwing an eye fillet onto the barbecue. It's sure to get a few oohs and aahs from the assembled blokes as you casually flip it on. In fact, it's worth the expense for this reaction alone.

1 eye fillet of beef, about 1½ kg (3 lb)
1–2 tbsp olive oil
Salt and freshly ground black pepper

> Rub fillet all over with olive oil and salt and pepper and place onto a hot barbecue. Cook for a total of 30 minutes, turning regularly. This involves rolling the fillet over a little (a quarter turn) every 10 minutes or so. This will produce a fillet that has been cooked to medium–rare. For a medium fillet, cook for a further 10 minutes.

> Allow the fillet to rest in a cool part of the barbecue for 10 minutes. Slice fillet and serve.

Serves 6–8.

[Note: if you are using a marinade or baste, simply brush this on a few times on each side as it cooks. There will be no need to use the olive oil, salt and pepper.]

CHILLI AND GARLIC MARINADE

This chilli and garlic marinade is just the treatment a fillet of beef deserves. As the beef cooks it forms a crust on the outside that tastes incredible.

1 large red chilli, de-seeded and finely diced
2 garlic cloves, crushed
1 tsp freshly ground black pepper
½ tsp sea salt
2 tbsp olive oil

> Mix chilli, garlic, pepper, salt and oil together. Rub over fillet and marinate for 30 minutes.

BARBECUE LEG OF LAMB

The Australian leg of lamb is, to my way of thinking, the classic meat for the Aussie barbecue. It always looks impressive as it's placed on the barbecue. It can cope with virtually every marinade or baste you can imagine and you get to carve it, which shows off your skill with a carving knife as well as the tongs. For lamb to cook evenly, ask your butcher to have it boned. This is what butchers call a butterflied leg of lamb.

1 leg of lamb, approximately 1½ kg (3 lb), butterflied
1–2 tbsp olive oil
Salt and freshly ground black pepper

> Rub lamb all over with olive oil and salt and pepper and place onto a hot barbecue.

> Cover and cook for 15 minutes, rotating as required. Turn lamb over and re-cover. Cook for a further 15 minutes, rotating as required.

> Remove lid and cook uncovered for 10 minutes. Allow the lamb to rest in a cool part of the barbecue for 10 minutes before serving. To serve carve lamb into thick slices

Serves 6.

[Note: if you are using a marinade or baste, simply brush this on a few times on each side as it cooks. There will be no need to use the olive oil, salt and pepper.]

LEMON, GARLIC AND HERB BASTE

Lamb comes up a treat when lovingly brushed with a baste such as this one here. It'll smell incredibly good too.

3 tbsp olive oil
3 tbsp lemon juice
3 garlic cloves, crushed
½ cup chopped basil, oregano and parsley leaves
Salt and freshly ground black pepper

> Mix together oil, lemon juice, garlic, herbs, salt and pepper. Brush onto your lamb a few times on each side as it barbecues.

BARBECUE PORK

Pork is one of the best meats to barbecue for lots of different reasons. It has just enough natural fat to ensure it will not dry our while cooking. It also copes well with virtually any flavour you care to marinate it with – particularly those with Asian ingredients or spices. Besides pork neck and leg of pork, belly pork is also a good cut to barbecue.

1–1½ kg (2–3 lb) pork neck or leg of pork
1–2 tbsp olive oil
Salt and freshly ground black pepper

> Rub pork all over with olive oil and salt and pepper and place onto a hot barbecue.

> Cover pork and cook for 15 minutes, rotating as required. Turn pork over and re-cover. Cook for a further 15 minutes, rotating as required.

> Remove lid and cook uncovered for 20 minutes.

> Allow the pork to rest in a cool part of the barbecue for 10 minutes before serving. To serve carve into thick slices

Serves 6.

[Note: if you are using a marinade or baste, simply brush this on a few times on each side as it cooks. There will be no need to use the olive oil, salt and pepper.]

SWEET STICKY PORK BASTE

Delicious! If time permits, marinate the pork in it for 2–3 hours before cooking then baste a little more on as it cooks.

250 ml (8 fl oz) soy sauce
125 ml (4 fl oz) rice vinegar
2 tbsp honey
1 tsp sesame oil
2 garlic cloves, crushed
2 tsp grated ginger
2 tbsp hot bean paste, optional
½ tsp five spice powder

> Combine ingredients and use to marinate your pork, or just brush onto pork as it cooks.

BARBECUE WHOLE FISH

Cooking a whole fish can be one of the scariest 'whole things' to cook on a barbecue, mostly because of the thought that it will fall apart as it cooks or that it'll end up dry. Neither of these things will happen if you choose the right fish and cook it properly – you're just going to have to trust me on this one. The best fish to use are firm fish such as snapper and Atlantic salmon. The fish can be wrapped in foil or banana leaves to help hold it together. This will also produce a moister fish, as it will steam as it cooks. Once mastered, try cooking it without foil or banana leaves.

1 whole fish, approx 1 kg (2 lb), gutted
1–2 tbsp olive oil
Salt and freshly ground black pepper
Banana leaves or aluminium foil

> Slash sides of fish diagonally 3–4 times. Rub fish all over with olive oil and salt and pepper. Wrap fish tightly in the banana leaves or aluminium foil. If using banana leaves you may need to tie it tightly with string to hold it together.

> Place wrapped fish onto a medium heat barbecue. Cover fish with a lid and cook for 20 minutes, rotating as required.

> Turn fish over and re-cover with the lid. Cook for a further 15 minutes, rotating as required.

> Remove lid and place fish onto a platter, unwrap gently and serve immediately.

Serves 4–6.

[Note: your fish can be flavoured from the inside as it cooks by placing a sliced lime, herbs and a few slices of ginger into the cavity before wrapping it up.]

BARBECUE WHOLE SMOKY SALMON

I've lost count of the number of times I've cooked a salmon this way, and every time it's a huge success. It has to be done in a kettle barbecue so you can add a few handfuls of smoking chips to the coals to get the authentic smoky aroma. This ensures the fish is virtually hot smoked in the barbecue, which in a way is getting back to the real origins of barbecuing (you've got to love that!). At first, the barbecue will send out plumes of smoke. Don't worry: this is an entirely normal part of the hot smoking method.

1 whole salmon or ocean trout,
   approx 2–3 kg (4–6 lb), gutted
1–2 tbsp olive oil
Salt and freshly ground black pepper
200 g (7 oz) mesquite wood chips, soaked
   in cold water for 15 minutes
A flat baking tray or a piece of aluminium
   foil 60 cm (2 ft) x 30 cm (1 ft)

> Prepare your kettle barbecue in the normal manner. When the coals have turned to white ash, place damp smoking chips on top.

> Rub fish all over with olive oil and salt and pepper. Lay the whole fish onto your baking tray or a piece of foil and place it in the hot barbecue. Place lid on the barbecue and cook for one hour, or until it is just cooked through. Serve immediately.

Serves 8–10.

THE SPIT ROAST

This is it: the ultimate barbecuing experience. This is a style of cooking where bigger is always better. I think of the spit roast as the V8 Holden Ute of the cooking world, replete with extractors, mag wheels and GT stripes. It's the ultimate barbecue power trip, and it all happens in the privacy of your own backyard.

Spit roasting is fundamental barbecuing at it's best. This is where the link between modern man and his ancient ancestors comes full circle; where modern man gets back to his pre-historic roots: cooking whole animals on a pole over an open fire.

This is one of our few chances to light a fire and tend to it until it has been reduced to a bed of glowing coals. It's where you get to impale a whole animal and gently cook it until it's tender, juicy and succulent. Finally the beast is carved and served to the waiting tribe. Sound familiar? Get your tastebuds jumping? You bet it does.

But first, a word of warning: there are many skills required to cook the perfect spit roast, all of which need to be mastered before cooking in front of a

I think of the spit roast as the V8 Holden Ute of the cooking world, replete with extractors, mag wheels and GT stripes. It's the ultimate barbecue power trip, and it all happens in the privacy of your own backyard.

crowd. Making and tending to a fire is a skill in itself as the coals must be kept glowing evenly under the animal. Then, as fat drips from the meat it will cause many flare-ups that must be controlled ASAP or they'll burn the outside of the meat. Also, as the animal cooks it will shrink slightly and may become loose on the rod, so you have to be ready with pliers, hammer and shifters to tighten it as it's cooking. Finally, there's the skill in knowing just when it's ready and how to carve it properly.

This is not a job for amateurs. The skills required are those that can only – and I mean *only* – be learned through practice and by starting with the basics of barbecuing.

SETTING UP

The following guide will provide all the instructions needed to prepare your fire for ideal barbecuing. It will take around two hours to get to this stage.

You will need the following:

A spit – somewhat essential to the whole process, I'm told. You can hire them from your local butcher or a catering hire company. They consist of the following components:

- A metal base, where the fire is made. Often this is a half-barrel or similar shape

- Legs, to raise the base off the ground and support the central rod to go across the fire

- A central rod (with attachments), to secure the animal. Without the attachments, the meat will not rotate correctly

- The spit must come with a small electric motor and a long belt to turn the rod during cooking

- Your spit roast should come with instructions on securing the animal to the main rod

Charcoal – a 2–3 kg (4–5 lb) bag should provide around 2–3 hours of cooking time. This is ample for a 15 kg (25 lb) lamb.

Firelighters – you'll probably need a 12–15 pack of firelighters for 2–3 kg of charcoal.

Long matches – it's possible that you'll need to re-light some sections of the fire. Long matches are essential as the radiant heat from the other coals can be quite intense.

Heat-proof gloves – a pair of sturdy, heat-proof gloves

are essential when lighting coals and for taking the rod off the hot spit.

A long handled shovel – indispensable when moving hot coals around in order to keep an even fire under the meat.

A water spray bottle – to deal with flare-ups as they occur.

A garden hose – it's very important to have a source of water on hand in case any embers should drift onto nearby grass or leaves.

FIRING UP

Set about 12 firelighters in the bottom of the spit and surround each with a mound of charcoal.

Light firelighters and mound charcoal around the top as they catch alight. Fan the flames well to ensure they catch.

You'll need a good, hot fire to get the charcoal to an appropriate temperature. When this stage is reached, add a second layer of charcoal and ensure it heats to the same temperature by fanning the flames well.

Be warned: this is a hot job. By the time you're finished, you'll end up smelling like a charcoal fire.

[Note: use a long handled shovel to move the coals around as needed.]

SPIT ROAST LAMB

Sheep were one of the first animals to be domesticated and so were an obvious choice when an animal was to be sacrificed for a feast or tribal celebration. Today, lamb is still one of the most popular choices for an Australian spit roast. This recipe has rosemary and garlic inserted into the meat before cooking and is lovingly brushed with a lemon and herb baste as it cooks. Just one taste will easily cement your tribal position as a true king of the barbecue.

1 whole lamb, approx 15 kg (30 lb)
35 sprigs of rosemary
1 whole garlic, divided into cloves
   and each one peeled

> Push the rod from the spit through the lamb and secure it tightly with the attachments.

> Make deep slits all over the lamb – the shoulder and legs in particular. Push the rosemary sprigs and garlic slices deep into the slits (if not in deep enough they will pop out during cooking).

> Place the lamb over the glowing coals and connect the motor to the rod using the long belt. Plug in the motor and turn it on to begin the lamb rotating.

The first 30 minutes of cooking

> During this time, your main job will be to keep the coals glowing evenly by adding extra coals to cold spots or by relighting spots of the fire with firelighters and extra charcoal.

The second 30 minutes of cooking

> By this stage, the meat will be starting to cook and to drip some fat onto the fire. As this happens the coals will flare-up and possibly burn the meat. This is when the water spray bottle is essential. Use it to put out little spot fires as they occur, but be careful not to put the coals out. These flare-ups will require your full attention.

> The lamb may have shrunk a little during this time and if so, you may need to adjust the attachments holding the lamb to the rod to ensure it turns correctly. You may need to remove the lamb and the rod in order to do it properly. Tighten as needed then place the rod back onto the spit, allowing it to continue rotating.

The remaining cooking time

> Once all the flare-ups have finished you can begin slowly brushing the marinade over the lamb as it turns on the spit.

> Keep an eye on the coals as you may need to move some of them around with your shovel to ensure there is a good fire underneath the legs, which are the thickest part.

> Continue to cook for a further 1½ hours then test the meat to see if it is cooked. To do this, insert a knife into the thickest part of the meat, then remove it. If the juices that come from the cut are clear, the

meat is ready. If the juices are red, the meat needs more cooking.

> When the lamb is ready, wrap it in foil and allow it to rest for 20 minutes. Some spits come complete with raised hooks so you can suspend the meat over the coals without it cooking further.

> Unwrap the lamb and begin carving. This can be done directly from the spit, but is much easier if you place the lamb on a table, remove one leg at a time and carve each directly onto people's plates.

Serves 30–40 people.

GARLIC, LEMON AND HERB BASTE

6 garlic cloves, crushed
150 ml (5 fl oz) lemon juice
2 cups chopped herbs – parsley, basil, rosemary, thyme, oregano
4 tsp salt
4 tsp freshly ground black pepper
250 ml (8 fl oz) olive oil

> Mix together garlic, lemon juice, herbs, salt, pepper and olive oil.

VEGETARIAN FOOD

It's inevitable that one day even the most expert barbecue chef is going to have to tackle the thorny subject of cooking vegetables. Now, most caring, sharing modern males should be okay about pushing aside a few of the sizzling sausages or marinated lamb cutlets to make way for something like barbecue onions, cobs of corn or even a couple of mushrooms. They might, in fact, even taste pretty good.

This compulsion to eat vegetables has led some people to actually prefer vegetarian food to the usual carnivorous offerings. If this happens you're going to have to cook this food separately from any meat, fish

Most caring, sharing modern males should be okay about pushing aside a few of the sizzling sausages or marinated lamb cutlets to make way for something like barbecue onions, cobs of corn or even a couple of mushrooms. They might, in fact, even taste pretty good.

and seafood because if it cooks in the fat from these things, it won't be vegetarian any more.

This chapter is dedicated to making this challenge as painless as possible, while still allowing you to cook up a storm. It contains easy-to-make recipes such as classic vegetable burgers, chickpea and lentil burgers and even mushroom risotto cakes.

You might also like to do some further exploration of your own. Branch out with non-traditional barbecue vegies like pumpkin, radicchio lettuce or sweet potato. Vegetables are also excellent when brushed with some of the spicy marinades on pages 69–72. You never know, you may even get a taste for vegetarian food and give up meat completely. Only joking.

BARBECUE ONIONS

There's nothing quite like the aromas that come from onions cooking on the barbecue. If you love caramelised onions all you have to do is sprinkle a few spoonfuls of vinegar and brown sugar over your onions as they cook. Just make sure you stir them really well.

1 kg (2 lb) onions, sliced into 1 cm (½ in) rings
3 tbsp olive oil
Salt and freshly ground black pepper

> Toss onions with oil, salt and pepper. Spread the onions out over the entire surface of a hot barbecue plate.

> Reduce the heat to low and cook the onions for about 30 minutes, turning them often. Add extra oil if they seem a little dry.

Serves 6–8.

BARBECUE MUSHROOMS

Mushrooms are really easy to cook on the barbecue, and they take on a marvellously rich flavour as they cook. You'll have everyone coming back for more of these, guaranteed.

500 g (1 lb) mushrooms of your choice
3 tbsp olive oil
2 garlic cloves, crushed
Salt and freshly ground black pepper

> Wipe mushrooms with a damp cloth. Mix the mushrooms with the oil, garlic, salt and pepper. Toss everything together really well.

> Place mushrooms onto a hot barbecue. Cook them for 15 minutes, turning often. Add an extra drizzle of oil if required.

Serves 4–6.

BARBECUE POTATO WEDGES

Try these wedges and you'd swear you were eating fried potatoes instead of barbecued ones. These are brilliant with a perfectly cooked steak.

1 kg (2 lb) medium potatoes
2 tbsp olive oil
Salt and freshly ground black pepper

> Cook your potatoes in boiling water until tender. Drain them and allow them to cool. Cut into thick wedges and toss with olive oil, salt and pepper.

> Put the wedges onto a hot barbecue plate; turn regularly. Cook them for 10–15 minutes or until golden. Serve immediately.

Serves 4–6.

BARBECUE CORN COBS

Corn is a natural on the barbecue: all it needs is to be peeled then brushed with a little olive oil before cooking. If you're keen on a little spice, corn is great with a dusting of aromatic sweet paprika on the outside.

3 corn cobs
3 tbsp olive oil

> Peel the corn cobs and make sure all the silky tassels have been removed. Cut each cob into 3 thick slices and rub with olive oil. Place the corn slices onto a hot barbecue and cook for 10–15 minutes, turning often.

Serves 4.

BARBECUE VEGETABLE BURGERS

These veggie burgers are held together with lots of mashed potato. Children love them, which makes a nice change from the age-old sausage in bread.

750 g (1½ lb) waxy potatoes, peeled
25 g (¾ oz) butter
3 tbsp olive oil
1 onion, finely diced
½ red capsicum, finely diced
1 small carrot, finely diced
1 small zucchini, finely diced
3 tbsp chopped fresh herbs
Salt and freshly ground black pepper

> Boil potatoes until they are tender. Drain, mash well and stir with butter. Heat a saucepan over a medium heat. Add oil and diced vegetables and cook until tender. Stir vegetables into mashed potato and add herbs. Season to taste with salt and pepper. Divide the mix into 10 equal portions and shape into burgers.

> Place the vegetable burgers onto a hot barbecue plate and cook for 5–6 minutes, rotating as needed. Turn them over and cook for a further 5 minutes, rotating as needed.

Makes 10 burgers.

VEGETABLE KEBABS

Vegetable kebabs may seem like an old-fashioned idea, but when jazzed up with a few spices, they're perfect for modern tastes.

2 garlic cloves, crushed
½ tsp ground turmeric
½ tsp ground cardamom
1 tsp ground coriander
1 tsp ground cumin
Salt and freshly ground black pepper
3 tbsp olive oil
1 eggplant, cut into 2 cm (¾ in) chunks
1 red capsicum, cut into 2 cm (¾ in) chunks
1 onion, cut into wedges
1 zucchini, cut into 2 cm (¾ in) chunks
10 skewers

> Mix garlic, spices, salt, pepper and olive oil. Toss with the vegetables until coated. Marinate for 1 hour to allow the flavours to infuse.

> Thread vegetables onto the skewers. Put the kebabs onto a hot barbecue and cook for 15–20 minutes, turning 3–4 times.

Makes 10 kebabs.

BARBECUE CHICKPEA BURGERS

These sound like the sort of thing that would go down well in a hippy commune and not in an Aussie backyard. Go au naturale and give one a go – they taste pretty damn fine.

400 g (13 oz) tin of chickpeas
3 tbsp olive oil
4 onions, sliced
2 tsp ground cumin
2 tsp ground coriander
1 tsp sweet paprika
½ tsp chilli powder
1 egg
100–150 g (3–5 oz) breadcrumbs
Salt and freshly ground black pepper

> Drain chickpeas and soak in cold water for 1–2 hours to remove the tinny taste they often have. Drain and mash roughly.

> Heat a saucepan over medium heat and add oil, onions and spices. Cook together for 20 minutes on low heat, stirring often until onions are soft. Mix onions and chickpeas together, then add egg and breadcrumbs. Mix to combine and season with salt and pepper. Divide mix into 12 equal portions and shape into burgers.

> Place burgers onto a hot barbecue plate and cook for 5–6 minutes, rotating as needed. Turn them over and cook for a further 5 minutes, rotating as needed.

Makes 12 burgers.

BARBECUE LENTIL BURGERS

Whip up a batch of these for your vegetarian friends and they'll be begging you for the recipe, guaranteed. They're fantastic with mango chutney (page 175).

1 tbsp olive oil
1 onion, diced
1 tsp curry paste
200 g (7 oz) red lentils, washed
500 ml (1 pt) vegetable stock
2 tbsp chopped fresh herbs
125 g (4 oz) ricotta
100 g (3½ oz) breadcrumbs

> Heat a saucepan over medium heat, add oil and onions and cook until soft. Add curry paste and cook for a further 3–4 minutes, stirring often. Add lentils, stir well, and add enough stock to cover. Bring to the boil, reduce heat and cook for 15 minutes, adding more stock if it looks dry. Continue cooking until the lentils are tender and all of the liquid is absorbed. Allow lentils to cool.

> Place them in a bowl and add herbs, ricotta and breadcrumbs. Mix well to combine all the ingredients and season to taste.

> Divide the mix into 12 equal portions and shape into burgers. Place the burgers onto a hot barbecue plate and cook for 5–6 minutes, rotating as needed. Turn them over and cook for a further 5 minutes, rotating as needed.

Makes 12 burgers.

SALADS

Salads are unknown territory for the typical male barbecue host. He may know they usually consist of lettuce leaves, a bit of tomato, some cucumber and maybe even a few slices of beetroot, but that's as far as it goes.

This state of affair has come about because, at a barbecue, the invited guests (and typically it's the female variety) usually bring the salads.

Salads have also been known to magically appear in the kitchen, courtesy of the lady of the house. Men have not previously been in the 'need to know category' where salads are concerned.

In order to correct this missing piece of the barbecue jigsaw the following pages cover all the salad information the modern male barbecue host should know. It's the things about salads that your mother didn't teach you before you left home.

There's a brave new world of salads just waiting to be explored: go forth, where no man hath gone before.

These instructions will tell you how to make a couple of basic salads and a simple dressing to toss with them just before serving. These are salads to cover all occasions, especially those ones where guests turn up at your barbecue unannounced and empty-handed (don't you hate that?). If you can whip up an extra bowl or two of salad, you should have plenty of food to go around.

Salads can also be a base to serve barbecued meats on. For instance, a salad of lettuce, tomato, olives, wedges of boiled egg and boiled potato topped with a few tuna steaks. Even simpler is a bed of lettuce, cucumber and tomato topped with slices of barbecued chicken fillet and a dressing.

There's a brave new world of salads just waiting to be explored: go forth, where no man hath gone before.

SALAD BASICS

The simplest salads are just good, fresh leaves tossed with a few spoonfuls of dressing.

Most supermarkets now make it easy for you by selling bags of lettuce leaves that are already washed and ready to use. If you buy whole lettuces, you'll need to wash and dry the leaves really well. This keeps it crunchy and ensures that the dressing will stick to the leaves.

QUICK SALAD IDEAS

Here are a few quick ideas for salads. Quantities here are as an accompaniment and should serve 4–6.

TOMATO AND CUCUMBER SALAD

> Slice 6 tomatoes and 1 cucumber. Mix this with the 2 tbsp lemon juice, 2 tbsp of olive oil, and season with salt and freshly ground black pepper.

GREEN BEAN SALAD

> Trim the ends off 500 g (1 lb) of green beans and cook them in boiling water for 2 minutes. Rinse under cold running water. Drain well, place into a bowl and add 90 g (3 oz) crumbled feta cheese, a handful of toasted flaked almonds, 1 tablespoon of vinegar, 3 tbsp olive oil, plus salt and freshly ground black pepper. Toss together gently.

BEETROOT SALAD

> Cut the leaves off a bunch of baby beetroot. Place the beetroot in a saucepan of water and boil until tender. Drain and allow to cool. Peel the beetroot and cut into wedges or slices. Toss with enough red wine vinegar, salt and freshly ground black pepper to taste. This is a great alternative to tinned beetroot.

TOMATO AND WHITE BEAN SALAD

> Drain a 400 g (13 oz) tin of cannellini beans and rinse well under cold running water. Dice 3 ripe tomatoes, 1 small cucumber, a little onion and 1 tbsp chopped mint leaves with 2 tbsp lemon juice, 2 tbsp olive oil, a little salt and freshly ground black pepper. Stir all the ingredients together well.

ASIAN NOODLE SALAD

> Boil 125 g (4 oz) of noodles in plenty of boiling water for 6–8 minutes, then refresh under cold running water. Mix together 100 g (3½ oz) sliced snow peas, 1 sliced red capsicum, 1 grated carrot, 1 sliced cucumber and a few shredded Vietnamese mint leaves. Add the noodles and 2 tbsp lime juice, 1 tbsp fish sauce and 3 tbsp olive oil. Mix well.

ASIAN GREENS SALAD

> Mix together 150 g (5 oz) washed baby bok choy, ½ cup coriander leaves, 1 sliced red capsicum and ¼ cup sliced spring onions with 1 tbsp lime juice, 1 tsp fish sauce and 3 tbsp olive oil. Mix well.

SALAD DRESSING

This is a stock standard salad dressing: an easy mix of one part vinegar to three parts olive oil. You can easily jazz it up by adding other flavours such as mustard, herbs or even chilli. Go on, experiment a little.

2 tbsp sherry or balsamic vinegar
6 tbsp olive oil
Salt and freshly ground black pepper

> Lightly whisk the ingredients together in a bowl.

[Note: one of the easiest ways of having dressing on hand is to make a large batch in a jar and keep it in the cupboard. Then all you have to do is shake the jar well and drizzle it onto your salad as needed.]

GREEN SALAD

Calling something a green salad doesn't mean all the lettuces have to be green – it's just the name for a salad made from fresh ingredients.

250 g (8 oz) lettuce leaves, washed
1 small cucumber, peeled and sliced
1 tbsp red wine vinegar
½ tsp mustard
Salt and freshly ground black pepper
3 tbsp extra virgin olive oil

> Toss salad leaves and cucumber together. Mix together vinegar, mustard, salt and pepper. Add oil and whisk well. Toss dressing through salad.

Serves 6.

GREEK SALAD

The Greek salad is a much-loved dish at all Aussie barbecues. Ideal with barbecued lamb and fish.

1 small cucumber, peeled and sliced thinly
½ red capsicum, diced into 1 cm (½ in) squares.
200 g (7 oz) feta, diced into 1 cm (½ in) squares.
3 ripe tomatoes, cut into wedges
½ red onion, thinly sliced
1 cos lettuce, washed
90 g (3 oz) kalamata olives
2 tbsp chopped parsley
1½ tbsp lemon juice
Salt and freshly ground black pepper
3 tbsp extra virgin olive oil

> Mix the cucumber, capsicum and feta with the tomatoes, onion, lettuce, olives and parsley in a bowl.

> Whisk lemon juice, salt and pepper together. Add oil and whisk well. Toss dressing through the salad.

Serves 6.

POTATO SALAD

How could you possible think of having a barbecue without a potato salad? It's the perfect match with sausages, steak and barbecue lamb cutlets.

1½ kg (3 lb) waxy potatoes, peeled
100 ml (3½ fl oz) mayonnaise
3 tbsp chopped flat leaf parsley
Freshly ground black pepper

> Boil potatoes until just cooked. Drain and allow to cool.

> Cut into 1 cm (½ in) slices. Arrange the potato slices on a platter. Drizzle with mayonnaise and sprinkle with parsley and freshly ground black pepper to serve.

Serves 6.

BARBECUED VEGETABLE SALAD

The beauty of this salad is it shows once and for all that the barbecue chef can do much more than just cook steaks and chops.

1 eggplant, cut into 8 wedges
2 small zucchini, cut into quarters
1 red capsicum, de-seeded and cut into 6 wedges
90 g (3 oz) button mushrooms
3 tbsp olive oil
1 tbsp vinegar
Salt and freshly ground black pepper
20 basil leaves, thinly sliced

> Place all of the prepared vegetables in a bowl. Add the olive oil, vinegar, salt and pepper. Toss well.

> Place vegetables onto a hot barbecue and cook for 20–30 minutes. Turn the vegetables regularly and add more oil if needed.

> When all the vegetables are tender and golden, pile them onto a platter. Sprinkle basil on top and drizzle on a little extra olive oil if it looks dry.

Serves 6–8.

PASTA SALAD

Pasta salad is almost as essential as the potato salad at Aussie barbecues. This is my own version of pasta salad and it brings pesto, mayonnaise and roasted vegetables into the equation. Try it just once and there'll be no going back.

500 g (1 lb) pasta (penne or spirals are ideal)
4 tbsp pesto
4 tbsp mayonnaise
2 tbsp cream
1 eggplant, cut into chunks
2 small zucchini, cut into chunks
1 red capsicum, de-seeded and cut into chunks
90 g (3 oz) button mushrooms, cut in half
3 tbsp olive oil
1 tbsp sherry or balsamic vinegar
Salt and freshly ground black pepper,
2 tbsp chopped chives

> Cook the pasta in boiling water until just softened. Drain well and allow to cool. Mix pasta with the pesto, mayonnaise and cream. Place all of the prepared vegetables in a bowl. Add the olive oil, vinegar, salt and pepper. Toss well.

> Place vegetables onto a hot barbecue plate and cook for 15–20 minutes, remembering to stir them well. Allow vegetables to cool. Mix the pasta with the barbecued vegetables. Place in a serving bowl then sprinkle with chopped chives.

Serves 8–10.

SALSAS, CHUTNEYS, SAUCES AND MUSTARD

Relishes and sauces can be the icing on the cake when it comes to the eating part of your barbecue. They can be the jewel in the crown of you barbecue success, your secret weapon to ensure your position as King of the Grill in your backyard– but only if you made it yourself.

Just imagine: you've barbecued a couple of rump steaks until they're perfectly cooked on the outside and packed with pink, meaty juices inside. These are a damn fine lunch as is, but served with a dollop of your own barbecue sauce or spicy chutney and your guests will be coming back for seconds ... and thirds ...

Even if you're not a master chef (don't worry, you will be), you'll find that most of these recipes are really easy to make. They go to prove that cooking is not rocket science, just common sense. Salsas are the simplest thing of all, just a mix of chopped vegetables with herbs, olive oil and vinegar, spooned over meat or fish when it is about to be served. Easy as pie really.

Chutneys and sauces (including barbecue sauce) are fairly straightforward too – mostly just a saucepan with some fresh or dried fruit, a few spices, sugar and vinegar in it. All you do is cook it until it's nice and thick then pour it into a jar or plastic container.

Even if you're not a master chef (don't worry, you will be), you'll find that most of these recipes are really easy to make. They go to prove that cooking is not rocket science, just common sense.

Also worth a try is mustard. All you need to do is soak mustard seeds for a day or two, then whiz the mixture in a food processor. You could also experiment with throwing in a few walnuts, a handful of fresh herbs or a chilli or two, as you please.

If you can see yourself smearing some of your own mustard onto a sizzling steak, or spooning a dollop of homemade sweet chilli sauce onto some lamb cutlets, it's time to get started.

TOMATO AND FRESH HERB SALSA

Salsas are incredibly easy to make. They are a good way to jazz up simple barbecued food like chicken, barbecued fish or prawn kebabs.

4 ripe tomatoes, diced
1 small cucumber, diced
6 basil leaves, thinly sliced
A few drops of sherry or balsamic vinegar
A few drops of olive oil
Salt and freshly ground black pepper

> Mix tomato and cucumber with the basil, vinegar and olive oil. Add salt and pepper as needed.

> Spoon over barbecued meats and seafood as preferred.

Serves 4–6.

MANGO CHUTNEY

Mango chutney is the sort of thing I find is perfect with barbecued chicken or pork. If there are no fresh mangoes in your local fruit and vegetable shop, you can just as easily use tinned mangoes that have been drained of their juices.

150 ml (5 fl oz) white wine vinegar
100 g (3½ oz) brown sugar
1 onion, finely diced
4 garlic cloves
1 tsp ground ginger
4 mangoes, peeled and chopped

> Place the vinegar, sugar, onion, garlic and ginger into a saucepan. Bring it to the boil then reduce to a simmer. Allow the ingredients to cook like this for 30 minutes, stirring often. It should reduce by half.

> Then add the mango and cook for a further 15 minutes. Remove from the heat and purée in a food processor if still chunky. Pour into sterilised jars or a plastic container.

Makes 1¼ litres (2 pints).

Store in a cool, dark place for up to 6 months.

SPICY TOMATO CHUTNEY

This spicy chutney will add a real fiery burst of flavour wherever it is used. If this sounds like your kind of thing, make it now.

100 ml (3½ fl oz) vegetable oil
2 tsp brown mustard seeds
1 tsp grated ginger
3 garlic cloves, crushed
1 tbsp chilli paste (or more if you want it really hot)
1 tsp ground cumin
1 kg (2 lb) ripe tomatoes
100 ml (3½ fl oz) white wine vinegar
75 g (2½ oz) sugar
½ tsp salt

> Heat the oil over a medium heat in a saucepan. Add mustard seeds, ginger, garlic, chilli paste and cumin and stir well for 5–10 minutes. Then add the tomatoes, vinegar, sugar and salt. Reduce the heat to a simmer and cook for 1 hour.

> Remove from the heat, season to taste and pour into sterilised jars or a plastic container.

Makes 750 ml (24 fl oz).

Store in a cool, dark place for up to 6 months.

BARBECUE SAUCE
(ALSO KNOWN AS BIG AL'S SUPER SAUCE)

This is the ultimate in barbecue sauces. Use it liberally at all your barbecues. It beats the hell out of tomato sauce every time.

100 ml (3½ fl oz) tomato paste or sauce
2 tbsp Worcestershire sauce
2 tbsp red wine vinegar
4 tbsp brown sugar
4 tsp smooth mustard
2 garlic cloves, crushed
250 ml (8 fl oz) water
Salt and freshly ground black pepper

> Place all ingredients in a saucepan and bring to the boil. Reduce to a simmer and cook for 15 minutes. If it looks too thick just add a little more water. Adjust seasoning with salt and pepper.

> Remove from the heat and pour into sterilised jars or a plastic container.

Makes 300 ml (10 fl oz).

Keep refrigerated for up to 2 weeks.

SWEET CHILLI SAUCE

Most of us are familiar with the sweet chilli sauce off the shelf. Get a taste for this homemade variety and you'll never go back on the bottle again.

250 g (8 oz) red chillies
4 garlic cloves, crushed
400 ml (13 fl oz) water
220 g (7¼ oz) caster sugar
1 tbsp salt
1 tbsp white wine vinegar

> Cut the chillies in half lengthways then remove the seeds and white membrane from inside. Slice the chillies thinly then place them into a saucepan with the remaining ingredients. Bring this to the boil then reduce the heat to a simmer and cook for 30 minutes.

> Allow the sauce to cool slightly, then pour it into a food processor or blender. Whiz the sauce until it is thick and combined. Pour into sterilised jars or a plastic container.

Makes 300 ml (10 fl oz).

Keep refrigerated for up to one month.

[Note: the variety of chilli you use in this sauce will determine how hot it will be. For a medium heat look for cayenne, poblano or serrano chillies.]

HOMEMADE MUSTARD

This will make a full-flavoured seed mustard – perfect for smearing onto barbecued steaks, cutlets and spare ribs.

100 g (3½ oz) white mustard seeds
250 ml (8 fl oz) grape juice
100 ml (3½ fl oz) red wine vinegar
2 tsp salt

> Place mustard seeds, grape juice, vinegar and salt in a bowl and allow to soak for 48 hours.

> Spoon the mix into a food processor or blender and process to a texture of your liking. Season with extra salt and pepper if required, or it may even need a pinch or two of sugar if it is very tart.

Makes 400 ml (13 fl oz).

Store in a cool, dark place for up to 12 months.

[Note: your homemade mustard can easily have other flavours added to it. Try adding 75g (2½ oz) of roughly chopped walnuts and a few sage leaves. Alternatively, add 3–4 tablespoons of red wine and a small hot chilli.]

DESSERTS

Desserts, not unlike salads, are the sort of thing that other people tend to bring to your barbecue. You never really have to think about them too much: they just turn up, covered in cream, sliced and ready to go.

The problem with this is that you never really know what's going to appear. It could be something rich like a huge pavlova, a chocolate cake or a cheesecake, or as simple as a fruit platter.

This is fine if you're really not that interested in making or eating desserts yourself, which is understandable if you've been slaving away over a hot barbecue for an hour or two. But if you want to provide your guests with a better selection of desserts, there are a couple of ways this can be better managed.

Ask people who are good cooks to bring a dessert – you could even send a recipe from this book!

The first thing to do is to ask certain people to bring certain desserts. We all know people who are famous for making a specific dessert, so that's usually a good start. Next is to ask people who are good cooks to bring a dessert – you could even send a recipe from this book!

The selection of recipes here is quite small, but it covers all the classics that appear at Australian barbecues, as well as a few things that I'd like to see more of on my dessert table. Last (but not least) have a go at making a dessert yourself.

QUICK DESSERT IDEAS

PAVLOVA #1

> Buy a ready-made pavlova and spread with thick cream. Scatter a punnet of raspberries or strawberries on the top.

CHEESECAKE

> Buy a ready-made cheesecake and spread with thick cream. Spoon the pulp from three or four passionfruit on top.

FRUIT SALAD

> Buy a mix of fresh fruit like watermelon, rock melon, berries, peaches, bananas, apples, oranges and pears. Peel them as needed and cut into thick slices. Squeeze some lemon juice over the fruit so it won't go brown.

SPONGE CAKE

> Buy a sponge cake and cut it through the centre. Spread the bottom half with strawberry jam and thick cream. Replace top half and sprinkle with icing sugar.

BARBECUED BANANAS

> Leaving the skin on, cut long slices into bananas and sprinkle a little cinnamon and brown sugar inside. Cook the bananas in their skins on a hot barbecue for 10 minutes. Peel some of the skin away and pour in a little cream before serving.

BARBECUED PINEAPPLE

> Remove the peel from a whole pineapple and cut lengthways into 6 wedges. Cut the centre core from each wedge. Place 3 tbsp butter, 3 tbsp brown sugar, 1 tbsp rum and a large pinch of mixed spice into a small saucepan. Cook over a low heat until it melts and combines. Place the pineapple onto a (very) clean barbecue grill and brush with the brown sugar mixture. Cook on the grill for about 10 minutes, turning often. Serve with cream.

PAVLOVA #2

Pavlova is the traditional barbecue dessert. Make sure there is at least one at your next sizzling event.

6 egg whites
440 g (15 oz) caster sugar
1 tsp vanilla extract
1 tbsp cornflour
1½ tsp white vinegar
250 ml whipping cream
Pulp from 6 passionfruit
200 g (7 oz) raspberries

> Preheat oven to 180°C (390°F). Beat egg whites until stiff peaks form. Add sugar, ⅓ at a time, allowing each third to be well incorporated so that you end up with a thick glossy meringue. Fold through the vanilla, cornflour and vinegar.

> Either spoon into a greased and lined 23 cm (9 in) springform cake tin or spread in a high circle on a sheet of baking paper on a tray. Place into oven and lower temperature to 120°C (245°F). Bake for 45 minutes. Turn the oven off, leaving the pavlova to cool inside the oven.

> Place cold pavlova on a serving platter and cover with whipped cream. Scoop passionfruit pulp on top and scatter with raspberries.

Serves 8–10.

SUMMER PUDDING

Summer pudding is an old-fashioned English berry dessert and it's just the sort of thing to serve at the end of a barbecue on a hot summer's day.

10–15 slices day-old white bread, crusts removed
500 g (1 lb) strawberries
200 g (7 oz) raspberries
200 g (7 oz) blackberries
200 g (7 oz) redcurrants
200 g (7 oz) loganberries
500 ml (1 pt) water
220 g (7⅔ oz) caster sugar
250 ml whipping cream

> Line the sides and bottom of a 1 litre (2 pt) pudding bowl with bread. Sort through the berries and remove any stalks. Bring water and sugar to the boil. Place berries and currants into this hot syrup and allow to heat through for 1 minute. Strain immediately, reserving the liquid.

> Return cooking liquid to the saucepan and boil until reduced by half. Allow fruit and syrup to cool completely before gently mixing the two together again.

> Spoon the fruit and syrup into the bread-lined pudding bowl. Add enough cooking syrup to cover, then top with more bread. Place a small plate on to the top of the pudding (one which fits inside the rim of the bowl). Put a heavy weight on it and refrigerate overnight (a heavy milk carton or two is perfect).

> To serve, remove pudding from bowl by placing a plate over the top of the bowl, turning it upside down and shaking gently until it comes out of the pudding bowl. Serve with whipped cream.

Serves 8–10.

NO-COOK ORANGE CHEESECAKE

Cheesecakes have a biscuit base with a delicious cream cheese topping. They need to be left in a refrigerator for a few hours to set.

150 g (5 oz) digestive biscuits
60 g (2 oz) melted butter
500 g (1 lb) soft cream cheese
150 g (5 oz) caster sugar
150 ml (5 fl oz) orange juice
10 g gelatine
100 ml (3½ fl oz) cream
Zest of 2 oranges

> Place biscuits in a food processor and whiz to form small crumbs, add melted butter and process briefly. Press biscuit mix into the bottom of a lined 20 cm (8 in) springform cake tin. Place in the refrigerator to set for at least 20 minutes.

> Beat cream cheese with sugar until well softened and creamy. Bring orange juice to the boil, add gelatine and stir until dissolved.

> Remove from the heat, add cream and orange zest and stir until fully combined, then stir it into the cream cheese mixture. Pour onto biscuit base and chill until set.

Serves 8–10.

TIRAMISU

This creamy, coffee-flavoured Italian trifle is just the sort of recipe to pass onto people who you know are good cooks when they ask what to bring.

4 eggs, separated
3 tbsp caster sugar
400 g (13 oz) mascarpone
3 tbsp sweet marsala
24 Italian sponge finger biscuits
125 ml (4 fl oz) strong black coffee
Cocoa powder, or grated chocolate

> Beat egg yolks with sugar until pale and creamy. Gently whisk in mascarpone and marsala. Whip egg whites until stiff then fold them into the mascarpone mix.

> Lay half the sponge fingers in the bottom of a large serving dish and drizzle with half of the coffee. Pour half of the mascarpone mix over. Add remaining biscuits and coffee and top with remaining mascarpone mix.

> Refrigerate for 3–4 hours to allow the flavours to fully develop. Sift cocoa or grate chocolate over the top before serving.

Serves 8–10.

CONVERSIONS

Measurements have been kept to a minimum in this book, however there are a few conversions that may make your life easier.

A teaspoon (tsp) is equal to 5 ml.

A tablespoon (tbsp) is equal to 20 ml.

LIST OF RECIPES BY SECTION

SPICE MIXES, MARINADES AND BASTES

New Orleans Cajun spice rub	67
North African spice mix	67
Chermoula spice mix	68
Chinese salt and pepper spice	68
Texan barbecue baste	69
Gutsy black bean and chilli marinade	69
Indian tandoori marinade	70
All-time favourite Texan baste	70
Oriental soy and garlic marinade	71
Caribbean fresh lime marinade	71
Lip-smacking lime and chilli marinade	72
Thai coconut curry baste	72

COOKING SAUSAGES AND BURGERS

Aussie Cevapcici	76
Beef burgers	77
Spiced beef burgers	78
Beef burgers with roasted vegetables	79
Thai chicken burgers	80
Chicken and veal burgers	81
Lamb kofta burgers	82
Veal and roasted capsicum burgers	83

COOKING ON THE BONE

Barbecue pork ribs	86
Texan pork ribs	87
Chinese pork ribs	88

Traditional lamb chops   89
Spiced lamb chops   90
Lip-smacking lime and chilli lamb cutlets   91
Texan chicken drumsticks   92
Thai coconut chicken chops   93
Chermoula chicken wings   94
Coriander, chilli and lime sardines   95
Minty salmon cutlets   96

COOKING KEBABS

Simple chicken kebabs   99
Chicken and prosciutto kebabs   100
Chicken tandoori kebabs   101
Rosemary lamb kebabs   102
North African spiced lamb kebabs   103
Classic beef, mushroom and capsicum kebabs   104
Chinese pork kebabs with black bean and sesame   105
Peppered kangaroo kebabs   106
Soy and ginger salmon kebabs   107
Tuna teriyaki kebabs   108
Cajun barbecued prawn kebabs   109
Bacon and scallop kebabs   110

COOKING THE PERFECT STEAK

Cooking the perfect porterhouse steak   114
Cooking the perfect rump steak   115
Cooking the perfect scotch fillet steak   116
Cooking the perfect T-bone steak   117
Cooking the perfect fillet steak   118
Cooking the perfect rib of beef   119
Japanese glazed steak   119
Chimichuri   120
Maple syrup and mustard glaze   120
Garlic butter #1   121
Garlic butter #2   121
Anchovy butter   122
Simple herb chicken fillets   123

Barbecue chicken salad 124
Barbecue beef salad with lime dressing 125
Chermoula spice salmon steaks 126
Barbecued fish fillets 127

COOKING WHOLE THINGS

Barbecue chicken 131
Garlic butter 132
Lemon and herb baste 132
Barbecue quail 133
Cumin and lemon baste 134
Barbecue duck 135
Japanese glaze 136
Tea-scented sticky duck marinade 136
Moroccan barbecued turkey 137
Barbecue fillet of beef 138
Chilli and garlic marinade 139
Barbecue leg of lamb 140
Lemon, garlic and herb baste 141
Barbecue pork 142
Sweet sticky pork baste 143
Barbecue whole fish 144
Barbecue whole smoky salmon 146

THE SPIT ROAST

Spit roast lamb 151
Garlic, lemon and herb baste 153

VEGETARIAN FOOD

Barbecue onions 156
Barbecue mushrooms 157
Barbecue potato wedges 158
Barbecue corn cobs 158
Barbecue vegetable burgers 159
Vegetable kebabs 160
Barbecue chickpea burgers 161
Barbecue lentil burgers 162

SALADS

Quick salad ideas   165–6
   Tomato and cucumber salad
   Green bean salad
   Beetroot salad
   Tomato and white bean salad
   Asian noodle salad
   Asian greens salad
Salad dressing   167
Green salad   167
Greek Salad   168
Potato salad   169
Barbecued vegetable salad   170
Pasta salad   171

SALSAS, CHUTNEYS, SAUCES AND MUSTARD

Tomato and fresh herb salsa   174
Mango chutney   175
Spicy tomato chutney   176
Barbecue sauce (also known as Big Al's super sauce)   177
Sweet chilli sauce   178
Homemade mustard   179

DESSERTS

Quick dessert ideas   181–2
   Pavlova #1
   Cheesecake
   Fruit salad
   Sponge cake
   Barbecued bananas
   Barbecued pineapple
   Pavlova #2   183
Summer pudding   184
No-cook orange cheesecake   186
Tiramisu   187

Campion & Curtis in the Kitchen

Campion and Curtis in the Kitchen is the new bible of Australian home cooking – whether you're stepping into the kitchen for the first time or looking for new ideas to rework your old favourites.

'The new bible of Australian home cooking.'

The Canberra Times

'Reminds me of much-loved books by Elizabeth David, Jane Grigson and our own Margaret Fulton.'

Divine magazine

AVAILABLE AT ALL GOOD BOOKSTORES